" THE CHINESE WILL EAT YOUR DOGS "

A handbook bringing into question 16 preconceived ideas on
China

« The Chinese will eat your dogs »

"To my family and friends, both Chinese and French. I hope to be worthy of you all in my thoughts as in my acts."

International copyright

July 2018

First version released (original text in French)

November 2018

Translated from French (original text + addendums)

January 2020

« The Chinese will eat your dogs »

INTRODUCTION – THE REASON BEHIND THIS BOOK

Nowadays is an exciting period.

I was born in Provence, in a village far from agitation and any foreign influence, with the exception of tourists coming by, most of them being English on bikes or Dutch with vans.

Growing up there was very pleasant, far from noise and fury, the crowd and the rat race, following the course of seasons interrupted by the 'mistral' north wind in winter and the persisting song of cicadas during long summers. However my destiny was to bring me far from all that.

As a major part of my age group, I inevitably left my region to go on with my studies and professional practice. Very early I decided to study finance. First perhaps by mere opportunism but also by inclination, I was then propelled to Paris as soon as the end of 2010 after a short stay in London, where I started to work for a large Anglo-Saxon investment bank.

In spite of Cassandra-like defeatists' judgement, Paris remains a global city firmly anchored in this new century. Paying attention to it while strolling in the streets, not just in touristic areas, one can hear more foreign languages than French and today Chinese even more than English. It may seem unimportant, but it struck me as years go by.

In spite of the pervasive pessimism of the French natives, quite understandable on some points, but remaining a Gallic characteristic associated with permanent criticism, Paris is a connected city specially with Asia. Since 2017, the change of government has already reconciled international investors with France and that can but improve after the socialist period which had badly impacted the image of the country. A new economic start and the adaptation to globalization that had long been rejected, will take place with the help of a better communication, which the 'Philippe' government put in place in 2017 is perfectly aware of.

A lot of Chinese are to be found among the international investors attracted by France. The frantic development of their country since the 1980s has created fantastic fortunes and huge international concerns, but China and its investors are still not warmly welcomed in France.

Being aware of the world new economic reality I have noted day after day in my job, with today a world changing from a superpower relatively declining to another gaining more and more confidence, I have decided to learn Chinese as soon as 2011. In my opinion that decision was totally justified at least for its economic aspect, a decision which more and more young French are making: in 8 years the share of China in the world wealth production went from 9% to 15%. China's GDP almost doubled between 2010 and 2016: a progression of more than 5,000 bn€ (+84%), being the equivalent of two years of French GDP according to the World Bank. And three years ago, the Asiatic giant has become the first economic power in the world in ppp (purchasing power parity); it's just the beginning of a fantastic story and the most dashing social and economic development our world has known within living memory. In spite of some doubts concerning the figures of the Chinese growth, maybe lacking precision, the difference from a year to another remains clear and the wealth of the Chinese people is improving : one just has to come back to the same place in China every year to see an enormous difference and changes that would have taken ten years or more in France to take shape.

It was about 8 years ago that I first travelled to China for nonprofessional reasons to meet those who were to become my future family in law. It was an unexpected encounter in the wonderful world of international finance during a cold November day which determined what would be my daily life during all the next years. As in all family stories there was a good deal of chance, but what followed later was just positive and enabled me, a young French man of multi European stock, coming from a region out of influential business circles, to have a seat in the first rank to see China's new development. Just the place to be, at the beginning of the 21st century, sometimes as an actor, most of the time as an observer. An experience of everyday, multinational and multicultural, sometimes difficult and demanding some implication, adaptation and constant tolerance, but so enriching on all plans. A permanent source of apprenticeship and, first of all, a means to have a different view on contemporary challenges.

From my travels, encounters, various discussions and observations I have noted (manners and customs on a personal plan or in business matters), I have made up a kind of mini dictionary on attitudes to adopt in China or with Chinese. My wife, my family in law and our Chinese friends have been a great help in that apprenticeship and I thank them a lot for their patience and their great kindness. I feel like getting into a rather secret world or at least closed to most people. Not like everybody, I had the idea or, better, I dared to write down a few reflections, ending with composing this handbook which, I think, is to be taken as an essay by essence far from perfect. In these few pages, I will try, sometimes humorously, sometimes more rigorously, now and then with some provocative remarks, to analyse some everyday life or cultural situations and find the right words to express the place of China in our contemporary world. A place different from yesterday's which will no longer be the same tomorrow despite the opposition of a part of the old world.

My frame will be an analysis by themes: every chapter is dedicated to a preconceived idea or prejudice, without any filter, the title expressing it as commonly heard among us. Of course those prejudices are to be taken on a second degree scale but they really express negative a-priori statements to be found in the French popular imaginary thoughts and, by extension, European and western: Chinese people would live in rabbit holes, would do nothing but work, would live apart from local life and so on... All subjects are taken into account, even those considered as non-politically correct, especially the latter I should say.

I hope this book, based on research, personal experience, local people testimonies, will enable to build bridges rather than walls between our two cultures, I daresay our two civilizations.

As a conclusion and before starting on all those points, I'll just add a few words on China, the western block and Europe in the first place : we live a difficult period concerning our identity because of migrations, of family links becoming more complex and sometimes transnational, or more simply because of a professional universe more and more mobile and open to the world. Everyone can have a multiform identity. It's my case.

Naturally I like China a lot and its people deserving admiration, which gave birth to this essay. But for other reasons I am also personally deeply attached to the United States and the north American culture. I am at last and before all European by birth and culture. But I contest the direction taken by Europe today, exclusively turned to an Atlantic alliance, a sort of western union. To my mind Europe should be a link between Asia, the Americas and even Africa. Our old Europe has all known since prehistoric times, all technical evolutions, all political regimes, it is the cradle of democracy, it has known all revolutions, either social or industrial. Its countries have engendered great discoverers and have brought a lot to the whole world. But they also have settled colonization before ending with decolonization after the second world war. Its peoples have committed irreparable things in fratricidal and suicidal wars, but, after that, a unique feat in the world, they also have achieved to make peace and unite strongly in the ties of brotherhood. Such is Europe of the second half of the 20th century and the 21st century. Some wisdom acquired with time which can today be a real link between civilizations. A link as an example. But for that we have to understand each other and drop prejudices. It's the first necessary stage. The lot of us, as western people, have a bad knowledge of Asia and too many "clichés" survive. The aim of this book is again very simple: to put an end to the prejudices mentioned and bring everybody to understand more and a little better, that country full of contrasts and paradoxes, that is China today.

TABLE OF CHAPTERS

« The Chinese will eat your dogs »

« The Chinese will eat your dogs »

1. "CHINA IS A DEVELOPING COUNTRY LIKE ANY OTHER BRICS"

Though the answer to this preconceived idea is maybe a little longer than to the others, as numerous aspects are concerned, it is interesting to introduce it first before meeting with less technical subjects. For some years now, more precisely since 2001, BRICs are a lot spoken of. This word coined with the first letters of the most important emerging powers, i.e. Brazil, Russia, India, China and South Africa, was invented by Goldman Sachs in a study that year in order to group those four gradually changing powers. As a fact, since the end of the cold war and the collapse of the soviet communist block, Russia is today generally classified among the emerging countries (even if the old concepts like the North-South border, so cherished by the French national education system but practically obsolete today, always consider Russia as belonging to the old industrialized countries).

That BRIC concept, later becoming BRICS (with the addition of South Africa) in 2011 and even today BRICSAM (for eccentric people adding Mexico to that imbroglio), was thus thought as a means to regroup those nations and consider them as belonging to a similar entity.

Of course the so-called BRICS countries have themselves used that term which enabled them to be better known and get more credibility in the international financial and political world, so much so as to create the first BRICS summits in 2009, eight years after the creation of the concept. But it was more a way of surfing on the bubble of reputation created after the Goldman Sachs study than showing a real unity of interests, even if the interests defended by a country like China are probably closer to those defended by a country like Russia than by the USA for example.

Finally, in my opinion, that BRICS concept is just a marketing term, in spite of the creation of a few very limited tools, like a common bank of development (in Shanghai) or still a reserve fund obviously unable to compete with the IMF (International Monetary Fund) of 189 member countries in use since the end of the second world war.

The BRICS are extremely various countries on all points. With the exception of some growth rates compared with the old European and North American already industrialized countries, what common points can we find in that block? They are so different on all levels.

Concerning their demography first with countries like India whose population is bursting and others where it's stagnant, like China whose unique child policy, indeed more flexible today, had an unrivalled impact in history. Brought into operation by Deng Xiao Ping in 1979 that policy was the most authoritative to be imposed on a whole country especially when you consider the size of China with a population of more than 900 million inhabitants at the time. From that point of view, China is already a unique case in history. Such a fast demographic transition has never been seen with a reproduction rate from 6.38 children by woman in 1968 to 2.3 in 1982 when the single child policy was fully imposed. Today the reproduction rate is probably lower than 1.7 children by woman, which is below the replacement level. That policy so much criticized has undoubtedly been a major element at the origin of the speedy development of China. Without it, China's population would at least be equal to 2.5 billion people (with a slower fertility rate) which means 1,100 million people more: clearly it would have been utterly impossible to get out of their extreme poverty so many people. In spite of being criticized a lot, we have to consider that ethnic minorities were not concerned by the single child policy (refer to the later chapter on the subject) and we can't accuse the country of being partial to the Han major population at the expense of ethnic groups like Tibetan people or Uyghurs. As a last point we don't dare to imagine the impact on the environment of an addition of more than 1.1 billion Chinese concerning the natural resources of the country and the whole world…and the pollution level that Chinese towns would know with more population when their situation is already problematic today. So on numerous aspects we mustn't be afraid of declaring that the policy of the only child, however strict it may have been in individual cases, had positive effects for society. This, of course, is just the beginning of the story, and the ageing population will bring negative effects as we can see in Japan with a significant decrease of population. But this is another story, and, as it is, I am convinced that a limitation of population is a good thing for the environment and in the end will create a decrease favourable to the world. That aspect alone shows that China is unique among that incongruous BRICS group in the sense it was the only country able to take such decisions and to ensure they were applied.

After demography let's tackle the economic part. It is indeed very difficult to find any harmony inside the BRICS group on this subject, with very different growth levels in the past, present and future. China was able to increase its wealth production in a dynamic and stable way, whereas other countries are much more volatile with periods of development and strong recession like Brazil or South Africa. As for India, a lot of structural obstacles (still poor infrastructures, social immobility due to traditional caste system, access to basic services excluding a part of the population…) have for long handicapped the economic growth, though the current Prime Minister's work based on a real taxation and administrative revolution, trying to fight against underground economy and corruption, is beginning to bear fruit today. A striking example is how the BRICS economy is composed. For China the manufacturing sector which enabled a lightning growth for more than 30 years represent 40% of the Gross Domestic Product in 2016 whereas the tertiary sector (trade, services) is regularly increasing and represents now 52% of GDP the same year. In India those two sectors respectively count for 29% and 54% of GDP, but this breakdown is misleading: almost half the population in 2016 was working in agriculture (in China less than 30%).

	Agriculture (% GDP)	Agricult. jobs	Industry (% GDP)	Services (%GDPB)	Nominal GDP	GDP per capita	GDP growth 2016
Brazil	5%	15%	21%	73%	1 796 Md$	8,840 $	-3,6%
Russia	5%	7%	32%	63%	1 283 Md$	9,720 $	-0,2%
India	17%	44%	29%	54%	2 264 Md$	1,670 $	7,1%
China	9%	27%	40%	52%	11 199 Md$	8,250 $	6,7%
South Africa	2%	6%	29%	69%	295 Md$	5,490 $	0,3%

Data 2016, World Bank

NB: The President Xi just announced in its 2020 New Year address to the Nation that the Chinese GDP per capita is now reaching 10,000 USD.

The economic figures given above show the scale of the differences between the countries belonging to the so-called BRICS group. Even the dynamic growth rates, one of the great variables defended to belong (as future giants) to this group, are no longer respected in 2016 with economic realities so different between a Brazil in recession, a Russia in crisis and a dynamic Asia. In front of those facts I think we have to admit that grouping those nations inside the BRICS block has little sense.

Culturally now, the countries belonging to this group have nothing in common: how about comparing Brazil and South Africa? India and Russia? A comparison often made that may look the least illogical but still is lacking sense, is between India and China. To my mind this is indeed irrelevant: when in the former religious tradition (mainly Hindu with Muslim and Buddhist parts) and the caste system rule many aspects of society, it is not at all the case for the latter. On the contrary in China, the secular society has dramatically changed along the last half century, for the best and the worst. Traditions have diminished or disappeared, the condition of Women has radically improved. Social mobility is a reality for a more and more important part of the population belonging to the educated "elite" and today's urban middle class. Even people living in the countryside are less and less set aside, and among my acquaintances I have several examples of enormous fortunes made out of nothing and of a disadvantaged social environment. That flexibility does not exist in India, at least not yet or very little. What's more, here we have just mentioned the social aspects. But both countries are also very different in their religious, economic and environmental aspects.

At last, historically the 5 BRICS countries do not have the same specific strengths to show off. South Africa and India have always been rather absent from the international scene and great decisions taken in the world. It's also true for Brazil. In spite of those nations' economic weight, they weren't able to impose themselves culturally, militarily or through the influence of their "soft power", whereas China sees today her "soft power" come to life, especially in western countries disappointed by NATO's leadership and facing the aggressive attitude of a block refusing to give more place to multilateralism, or still in Africa where China is appreciated for the funds she grants for development without the political involvement of the old colonial powers. Among South Africa, Brazil and India, the latter is the only one having a true millenary history, and even if the present day country hasn't always existed as an entity, it has left its track in the History of humanity and has been an actor of its writing. As for Russia, compared to the rest of the BRICS, it takes advantage of being the direct heir of cold war and the USSR block. That country was a major actor in the world power relations of the 20th century and has kept its military development as one of the most important in the world. Russia has also greatly contributed to the global march on the political level and its example, at the time of communism, has shaped a lot of other nations. Now let's come back to our main subject: China is a country with a thousand-year-old history whose continuity both territorial and cultural, from antique days to now, is unique. We must not forget the heavy weight of the four great Chinese inventions i.e. paper, printing, compass and cannon powder on our own history, which, but for them, would have been modified and a lot of experiences and other western discoveries would have been compromised.

Let us not forget that, like the Muslim world in front of Europe at a time, or the Greeks and Romans in front of the barbarian tribes, China had a considerable advance on technical, scientific, social and economic plans before the Western world in the Middle ages and during Renaissance. At times we could almost qualify as prehistoric for Europe, China was already a political and cultural ensemble with a real administration open to scholars in a meritocratic approach by means of national exams, the most modern system in the world then. It is only in the 19th century and in the first part of the 20th that China lost its rank and was overwhelmed by Western powers as a consequence of the first and second industrial revolutions. It is precisely at that time that the Middle Kingdom, undermined by internal instabilities on political and social plans and economically short of breath in front of Western powers and the new modernized Japanese power, found itself almost totally under the domination of foreign countries by a sort of semi-colonization, or in a state of vassalage which did not dare to tell its name. Culturally the country today still keeps track of it and that episode has always been felt as a shame, China being reduced to a power of subordinate status, in front of people often acting brutally (the sacking of the Summer Palace by England and France to bring the government to change in the opium conflict) when they were considered as foreign barbarians. Squeezed in obsolete and corrupted institutions, unable to react before the ever increasing demands of European maritime powers, paralysed in front of the evolution of Japan that could adopt western techniques, China found itself in a position of inferiority and poverty which lasted more than a century. We might have thought the situation wouldn't change and western countries and Japan would always be dominating nations as our history books still suggest. But time does not elapse in the same way in a several thousand-year-old country. Truly, a century, compared with the long history of China, is just a short period of time, not more than 3% of its history. That's why, since the eighties, China catching up with its former competitors that have become its economic partners, is not meaningless. The situation isn't really new, though such a quick and massive economic recovery is unheard of in human history. It's rather the coming back to the fair place of China in the world than a major change. That coming back shouldn't be surprising for observers familiar with China, its history and culture. Let's mention a significant figure: between the 1st century AD and the 1st half of the 19th century, China has always represented from 22% to 33% of the wealth produced in the world (that we could compare to GDP today), which varied according to historical periods and the size of the Chinese empire but was always outstanding. What we can see today is just the end of a short chapter in the history of the country, a chapter which has lasted for 120 or 130 years. A long time for a young country like the USA but just a trifle for China.

As a conclusion, we can simply say it is not easy to make out the part of mystery concerning that country and it's not certain that one observer from the outside could be able to understand China as well as fully informed Chinese people. But one thing has to be stated clearly: it's not possible to include China in the anachronistic and dissimilar BRICS group, which is also true of the other countries, having each their own history and culture, and or course specific economic characteristics determined by their own opportunities and limitations. It's high time we did not include them in a group causing nothing else but confusion.

2. "CHINESE PEOPLE ARE IMPOLITE"

This is one of the criticisms made by many people alien to China (coming from western countries or not): Chinese people are impossible to take out as they are dirty, spit on the ground, knock into other people, shameless smoke throwing their stumps everywhere in the streets, don't use litter bins, well, are extremely impolite. This criticism, however simplistic it may be, is not wholly unjustified, for, it's true that some groups, out of China, have a bad behaviour and convey that kind of prejudice. That generalisation, once told, is a snap judgement coming from people with a limited knowledge of China and its natives and who, very often, never had any experience of life in the country. We have often heard of those anecdotes taking place during a travel in a foreign country while visiting a place where Chinese people were present. But that criticism concerning groups of Chinese visiting Paris for example, is much less often heard of.

Then, what about it? Are Chinese people really impolite as a country characteristic, or is it just a small minority of them?

First of all, it is very important to remember that all Chinese are not equal concerning education and good manners, or, at least, what is considered as such by us, western people. Once again China is a huge country with a lot of various cultures despite the overwhelming domination of the Han ethnic group (historic ethnic group of the Chinese people, named after the Han dynasty from 206 BC to 220 AD, which represents about 92% of the population of continental China in

2017). Today in rural areas there are still landlocked regions where life is very difficult. So it's more than restrictive to make generalizations on behaviour. There is a huge difference between a Chinese from Shanghai in his way of life and a Chinese living in a village from the province of Henan (a rural province I choose at random with a majority of Han people) because of a very different education and financial means equally situated at the opposite end. To draw a comparison, it's as if we linked the way of life and thinking of a well-off inhabitant of the wealthy districts west of Paris with someone who had spent his life as a sheep farmer in Lozère (very rural and beautiful department in central France). Or still if we compared a Frenchman (from a cultural and financial point of view) with an inhabitant of central Africa. In continent-size China we have differences and contrasts of this kind.

This being brought to mind, (we'll probably repeat it in this essay) we can now better understand the disparities existing in Chinese people's behaviour. I have personally noticed such inappropriate behaviour and we have all read articles in which people were surprised at or scandalized by the manners of some Chinese nationals. For instance, I personally remember a visit in a temple in Indonesia (more precisely in Bali), a lot of Chinese tourists being present. It's true they were noisy, without embarrassment (referring to my western standards of discretion, I should say French standards because some Anglo-Saxon people seem to be more tolerant to noise) and they smoked a lot which caused comments from other visitors who frowned at them, and I even heard an American tourist say "fxxxxxg Chinese" when she passed by them as they were taking a lot of space on the path, talking very loudly. Without mentioning ordinary racism, sad to say, totally assumed towards Chinese people, those reactions emphasize the gap and the lack of comprehension between groups of different nationalities. In front of such a behaviour which can be annoying (I confess it has sometimes got on my nerves) we must keep a sense of proportion: those incidents are rather rare and are caused by a minority of Chinese often from rural areas. As they have had no contact with people of external cultures, they don't realize their actions can be felt as impolite. Their fellows from urban areas are themselves uncompromising with them and don't tolerate their lapses of conduct, but those people living in their province have the same behaviour everywhere and can't understand clearly what they are accused of.

On the subject I can give a second striking example. It took place in 2012 or 2013 on a regular air service plane between Shanghai and Paris. On the plane there were several groups of Chinese travelling to Europe by an agency specialized in group travels. Such groups are sometimes made up of people coming from the countryside with all the features we have just mentioned. And some of those behaviours didn't fail to happen on the plane: very loud discussions, sudden unexpected movements, seats in a lying position at meal times as well as other unpleasant attitudes. I then realized the enormous differences existing between Chinese: apart from hostesses, many Chinese travelling alone admonished them and the passengers concerned changed their attitude; some of them were even roughly blamed and the rest of the flight could run smoothly.

Such behaviours are not deliberate: they are the consequence of a real cultural gap between western people and Chinese as well as between Chinese themselves. Those cultural differences come from education and with the arrival of new generations they are less and less to be observed. In 2019, I had the opportunity to feel the difference, in particular for flight travels where young Chinese are now more polite that western people. So I am confident in the fact that slowly the Chinese will be as known to be polite as Japanese or Korean people for example, though some differences in culture and education will probably be hard to get rid of. They still exist in our western world: is there a Frenchman who has never felt uneasy on the London tube at pubs closing time? Or in Spain late at night when local people start their meals and festivities outside when our French fellows would like to sleep? Or in Paris on the 'Grands Boulevards' in front of groups of Americans shouting in excitement at the tops of their voices? Those attitudes are not considered as impolite in their native culture and are not aimed at causing trouble, they are just cultural characteristics. Accepting them within reasonable limits shows our capacity of empathy and tolerance. It's exactly the same story between western and Chinese people.

Modern China didn't build itself in one day. It's still developing slowly and has changed a lot since its revolution and the communists led by Mao took power from the nationalists of Chiang Kai-shek. The population had to put up with deep economic and cultural upheavals and exactly like the French, during their own revolution more than two centuries ago, suffered the worst. Habits have been knocked over, very old cultures were wiped out, sacrificed on the altar of forced modernization and a new course of action in social and economic fields was adopted, roughly at times, by some parts of the population. It's also true for politeness or what we can consider as politeness according to our own foreign standards. Bad habits are still anchored in some rural areas where, for years in a closed circuit, was proclaimed the superiority of the country people over intellectuals, of the workers over the scientists, of extreme simplicity over sophistication. The contempt displayed by some leaders towards the old political system and classic social regulations did the rest, in addition to the lack of education that is still observed among some Chinese groups. Those people are always pushed out of mainstream and have not yet taken advantage of the new wealth of their country. As a consequence, we will usually come across them on low-cost destinations nearby like South-East Asia, always travelling in groups. Because of their locked position we must be aware that their life is still hard today in spite of their country's great jump forward: so we must not throw stones at them. They have just started opening themselves to the rest of the world, their life isn't easy, and I think we must give them a chance.

Since 2013, following a lot of scandals described with relish in our international medias (unlocking of plane doors before taking-off, dirty marks in hotels and other rejoicing actions) the Chinese government itself decided to tackle the problem. As a matter of fact we could read in our papers that a "guide of good manners" had been distributed in China by the power (National Administration for Tourism), so as to banish behaviours like "spitting in public, urinating in bottles or tagging historical places" as described in French papers like Le Figaro. Personally I couldn't get a look on that guide, but the then vice-prime minister, Wang Yang, declared that such manners were harmful for the "image of the Chinese people". That guide was not only a compilation of good manners for brutish tourists but also a cultural aid to help Chinese in foreign countries avoid some blunders (like offering chrysanthemum flowers at a dinner in France or asking for pork in a Muslim country). Of course, that guide can easily be cartooned and any Chinese citizen with some education has no need of it.

Moreover can we really criticize such behaviours when, in our own country, when sales promotions on Nutella (the famous sweetened hazelnut chocolate spread) or on children's diapers in supermarkets cause riots where, to obtain as many packets as possible, aged people are stepped on (seen several times on TV in 2017 and widely publicised by medias)? We also have to look at ourselves: I don't think I am less well placed culturally in France, however I confess that in my life I have transgressed the first two taboos of the guide and one day in Shanghai I have asked for a beer in an Uyghurs restaurant of Xinjiang cuisine as I hadn't even noticed it was a blunder…Errare humanum est.

As a summary, I think that what we consider as impolite when we come across Chinese in foreign countries has three main causes which could come from:

- The responsibility of revolutionary events which radically transformed China in the fifties and sixties. The population changed drastically during those two decades and the original Chinese mind was durably affected. It can be seen in historic buildings and in the inheritance of ancient China: unfortunately, there was a lot of mess on the altar of revolution. Good habits disappeared as well as bad ones and even if the situation has generally changed for the better today, China and its population have suffered from real cultural losses during that period when paradoxically they also have benefited from those rapid upheavals in economic terms.

- The difference of culture and education; as mentioned before, we western people have a different view on some attitudes. Some actions, considered as normal in various parts of China, will look detestable to us (speaking loudly, smoking, spitting noisily) where local people don't find fault with them. We also can behave rudely in China or with Chinese people unintentionally. At the restaurant in France dividing the bill seems normal but it's a serious offence (inviting people to do so means that one isn't generous or terribly stingy) in China where the guests invite each other in turn and sometimes quarrel (conventionally) to pay for the whole bill. In such circumstances I think the best is to point out the mistake without rebuking the person, just to help him behave better in the future in front of another culture. The Chinese are open-minded, and they generally don't judge foreigners. On the contrary they try to understand them and easily forgive their cultural blunders.

- The pressure of the population: a last factor, we haven't yet mentioned, and which plays a significant role, is the huge pressure of the population on individuals in China. Imagine that pressure in big cities like Shanghai, a special administrative area whose population is almost 25 million people in 2019. In those urban jungles one has to fight for everything : a seat on the underground railway, a reservation at the restaurant, a lane on the motorway…As a consequence the individuals have to adapt themselves: they push in waiting lines, try to skip the line…Once again those behaviours are not to be observed among the young educated generation who have always known that and patiently wait as in Japan or South-Korea. Nevertheless, the other Chinese acting so in their homeland have a tendency to do the same in foreign countries in a different context, which will be badly perceived by the local people.

As a conclusion, I think that those behaviours, sometimes real, sometimes overstated by our fellow citizens quickly judging Chinese people, will slowly disappear. On one hand, education and the government efforts are beginning to bear fruit. Today there are exhaustive brochures given by the government and travel agencies to some categories of population in China so as to explain in detail how to behave in foreign countries (no shouting, no pushing, no spitting…).

On the other hand, things are quickly changing in China. Differences tend to rub out fast thanks to the young generations. Even if it's not perfect, improvements are visible. To assert my view, I can speak of the high level of cleanliness in most developed cities. It's so clean that one could eat on the ground in many Shanghai or Beijing quarters. Of course, like everywhere, there are cases of incivility, but on the whole, it's cleaner than in Paris. Yes, in our country, who never stepped on a dog's dropping which its mistress so neat on herself didn't clean up? Or who wasn't indignant at a passer-by throwing his still lit cigarette stump almost on our shoes? Or still, when someone loudly spits on the pavement or empties his bladder in a corner after an evening too well watered? Those behaviours, sad to say, are universal, and it wouldn't occur to us to accuse all the French of those misbehaviours. It's in big cities as in China that things are changing. Those cities are pleasant and clean because the population isn't so undisciplined as we are made to believe. Electric scooters and cycles are everywhere (no sound or smell pollution, combustion engines are forbidden), China is a leader for bike-sharing system without stations (it works well in spite of some incivilities for parking places), recycling bins are everywhere as well as charging points for electric vehicles in all underground car parks…those are a few examples of new habits more ethical and more ecologic of Chinese citizens which leads us to our next chapter!

3.   "CHINA IS TOO POLLUTED"

This sentence has been said over and over, relayed by the media and sometimes by tourists coming back from China. Once more, as for other preconceived ideas, there is some truth in that statement, but I think it's both alarmist and inaccurate.

First, it's not whole China that is polluted. A country with such a size has an extremely important biodiversity and there are plenty of parks and natural spaces preserved in spite of a territory that concentrates more than 18% of the earth inhabitants on only 7% of emerged lands. When you consider the fact that China produces nearly 16% of the world wealth in 2017, it's a source of powerful constraints. What's more, China concentrates many delocalised polluting industries in their homeland to produce export goods, which will finally be of benefit to other countries. All of us, we often export our pollution to China through that mechanism.

So, if the whole of China isn't polluted, some towns really are. Let's speak first of atmospheric pollution, i.e. airborne particles. The most important cities like Beijing and Shanghai are not necessarily more impacted, but, it's more visible as they are more exposed in media and well-known by tourists. In fact, it's quite possible for people regularly going to Beijing to avoid pollution. Apparently, it's more important in winter (because of power plants still often coal-fired and linked with the heating systems) than in summer. I personally went to Beijing less than 10 times, for several days' stays and I think that one day out of three was polluted (probably one out of four during summer stays and half of them in wintertime). In Shanghai the atmospheric pollution or smog (a word coined at the time of the great London pollution in the 1950s when the mist of the Thames and the coal and industrial fumes mixed to form a thick fog) seems to be constant throughout the year, but it's more difficult to check with the naked eye than in Beijing. As a matter of fact, Shanghai has always been a misty region, especially during cool months, and it's easy, for badly informed people too quick to respond, to consider any fog as pollution. Aged Chinese told me that formerly people used to say "there is fog today" whereas nowadays they say "there's a lot of pollution". That confusion is more difficult in Beijing where the climate is much drier, though winds laden with sand from the northern desert areas sometimes sweep the city, giving a stronger feeling of pollution in the atmosphere. We mustn't forget that people also feel pollution not only in towns but chiefly in the countryside too, in areas next to factories and power plants.

Pollution is too often assimilated with that foggy atmosphere even when it's much more insidious: stream contamination, discharge of plastics, illegal dumping, various incivilities, outgassing of industries and so on. China, like other countries, doesn't escape the rule. Stream pollution is perhaps more problematic, as it is in moist environments that biodiversity is more developed as well as it is from rivers that water for human needs is drawn (and used for animal breeding and irrigation too) before being treated, not always satisfactorily. Everyone remembers those thousands of dead pigs infected by a disease in 2013 and thrown into the Huang Pu, an affluent of the

Yangtze, flowing across Shanghai. Maybe they came from a suspect farm whose owners wished to avoid sanctions: an incivility among others. The people involved in that contamination may have thought that the carcasses would be carried away to the sea? It's a pity that, in that case, their intellectual capacities were as low as their degree of hygiene. Another example, which is perhaps less shocking, is the water eutrophication of Tai Hu lake, the third freshwater lake in size in China, with a perimeter of 400km, near Shanghai in the province of Jiangsu. It suffered from the discharge of agricultural waste causing an explosion of nitrate level and a toxic algal bloom, slowly depriving the lake of oxygen and degrading the aquatic environment. I have personally observed it: though the place is beautiful and despite the efforts made recently, we can't help feeling it's a real mess. A plague among others that China has to face with, like a lot of countries, especially when they develop at a forced march. The population is aware of the problem. Otherwise why would they install air purifiers in their children's room? The government is aware of the problem too and proves it by trying to promote green energy (we'll deal with that subject later) but we must keep a sense of proportion. Indeed, the pollution level is problematic in several areas for a large part of the year, but some mist doesn't necessary means pollution. It's a misleading abridgement too often made by observers. A romantic winter fog in Paris (still having now and then important levels of pollution with particles) will be transformed into a toxic cloud of pollution in Shanghai, without taking account of the surveys not always made in good conditions. On this subject concerning China, let's not dramatize with flamboyant gestures as some media and political people do to serve their own interest. There's indeed a problem but it is not always pollution.

Now let's deal with green energy. How long will we focalize on pollution only, a reality regularly declining, rather than on positive aspects like renewable energies producing more and more electricity in the country? In 2017, 25% of electricity is produced by dams, windmills and biomass. In France it's less than 18% that same year, a level that seems to be stagnant for some time. Concerning solar energy, in 2016 photovoltaic capacity increased by 50% in the world and China accounted for about half of the growth (source: International Agency for Energy, 2017), no less! China is today the world leader in the production of electricity from renewable energies, at the first rank in hydroelectric generation, as they have invested a lot to build dams, at the first rank too in solar energy production since 2016 with 6 out of the 10 biggest solar industry firms and 20% of the world production, and ranks second for wind electricity generation (more than 20% of the world production here again). Of course, it doesn't erase the fact that China produces about 30% of the world greenhouse gas emissions, but the revolution is underway, and we have every cause to be happy about it. The peak of emissions is weakening, and some indicators show a gradual decrease, like the coal consumption getting down by 1% for the first time in 2014. In the near future China is even going to stop urban heating running on coal, to show their good will and signal the change to their own population.

So there is some hope and it's important to see the glass half full. China is still handicapped by its industry concentrating the manufacture of plenty of export goods. We must keep in mind that many countries in the world delocalize their pollution in China as well as their factories. But that pollution is a shared responsibility and it's too easy to cast opprobrium upon China with 30% of greenhouse gas. We mustn't forget that the population of China producing twice as much gas as the USA (being the second polluting country in the world) is 4.26 more numerous in 2017…When you consider the number of tonnes of CO_2 by inhabitant each year, China is much less greedy than Australia (16.9), the United-States (16.6), Saudi Arabia (16.6), Canada (15.7), South Korea (12.7), or Japan and Germany (more than 10). In fact, China isn't too bad a pupil with 7.4 tonnes, next to the average emissions in the European Union (7.3 tonnes), but to be objective it's true that we should compare countries with a similar GDP by inhabitant and a similar development level. Let's be wary of statistics hastily thrown on the table. We use them as we like and they are not interesting and fair elements of comparison.

To progress in this debate, I have to insist on the fact that, apart from the handicap of pollution widely criticized, China has immense advantages. Its territory first, enabling huge hydroelectric buildings, wind farms and photovoltaic panels. Its political regime too, on that specific aspect: unlike our democracies where decisions are long to be effective with countless legal appeals (a well-known problem in the construction sector), a political authoritarian regime has an advantage: very quick decisions on difficult questions. The green energy sector is in full bloom and, surprisingly, China leads the revolution. Its financial capacities and huge population are profitable in quantitative rankings. Nevertheless, it's important to tell it again: China isn't the biggest polluting country and the efforts made are slowly bearing fruit. Everything is being done in a lot of fields, to the credit of the country: economic landing, human development, a new image on the international scene, an expensive fight against pollution, demographic transition…Those are titanic challenges. It can make us think, and my opinion is that things will improve for the best, as China has a strategy and knows our history.

It's a clever strategy: gradual closure of coal-fired plants or other fossil energies that the country will still need for a few years, which were the base of its energy production to support growth. But such a closure can't be too sudden: we often think of China's growth in a relative level (or in a percentage of growth if you prefer) but when we consider it in an absolute mode, it's much more limpid: in 2017 the wealth produced by the country compared with 2016 was worth 970 billion U.S. dollars, which is almost 40% of France GDP, and it's the additional wealth produced by China in just one year! Nice jackpot indeed. So constraints are enormous for the country and what is in wait is unexpected: they can't allow themselves to sacrifice their growth. Thus, while waiting to close polluting plants, the government has chosen to invest massively in nuclear power-plants. At the beginning of 2018, China had 38 nuclear reactors and 20 were under construction. Those classical reactors, among the most modern in the world (the first EPR reactor is fully operational in China in 2019 whereas it is still not finished in France), will perhaps be completed by pharaonic projects of floating reactors currently under study but fraught with many difficulties. One might think nuclear plants are anti-ecologic because of the waste from fissile material, but, doing so, China kills two birds with one stone: 1/ they will highly reduce particles in the atmosphere and emissions of greenhouse gas to be considered as good pupils (a good strategy to improve their image in the world and to relieve their displeased population), and 2/ it will soon be Chinese firms instead of western firms like Areva (today Orano) which will sell nuclear technology throughout the world. The Chinese groups build up a significant experience for the future, unlike the historical groups in countries having very few projects or in which nuclear technology has been abandoned (Germany). This is a good method to clean up and get rid of opponents while strengthening their economic advantages: clever enough.

 At last, in addition to their two big actions, the Chinese strategy consists in getting on with their economic transition. In a recent past specialized in exports with all their polluting factories, China now tries to have a stable growth for their own benefit and a better environment, a growth which will now depend on internal consumption. Such a transition will mechanically result in a rate of growth less and less high, as the rate of human development is higher. Once more it can be considered as a good method to avoid economic inflation literally as well as figuratively.

I have said before that China knows history well. In my opinion they are going to prove it: let's remember what happened in the western world, in London, in the 1950s, the great smog period. For decades, the United Kingdom that had become a big industrialized country had been polluted by coal burning used for heating, industries and transports before the second industrial revolution. In 1952, as the winter was cold and without wind, London became a prey to a powerful episode. For 5 days a thick cloud of smoke remains floating in the air, and, as a consequence, 12,000 people die straight from that pollution, that is 1.5% of the whole population of Greater London at the time. In the sixties the river Thames was even declared "dead", biologically dead to be more precise according to the terms used by the British Natural History Museum in 1957. Nothing could survive in it and the muddy waves of the river were then described by the media as a disgusting and stinking open-air sewer. We are far from the situation observed in China today; however, nowadays, owing to measures taken for several decades with a better treatment of waste, dirty waters and industrial discharges, there are about 130 kinds of fish living in the Thames again and seals have come back. It means that no situation is hopeless. The Chinese government knows it well, and the people bow their backs during the necessary transition unfortunately imposed by our economic, capitalistic and polluting way of life. And sooner or later the good results will come.

The government is aware of it and takes action. Not only for altruistic reasons or out of environmental awareness, but also because, in China, excessive pollution and a lower quality of life are a factor of social instability. The Chinese political regime can maybe be blamed for a lot of things, and as all regimes it is far from being perfect, but an advantage, often forgotten, is that adapting itself to the population is a necessity. To maintain itself, a political regime can't rely on repression and must, to some extent, be supported by its population. It is a fact that a majority of Chinese citizens still support their government, but in front of pollution a lack of action can be dangerous as it's too risky for the health of families. Their relatives' safety comes first before patriotism and the government knows it well, as families are the priority in the Chinese society, contrary to a democratic system where electors can be content with demagogic promises (it's no use mentioning a lot of examples in Europe and North-America in 2012, 2016, 2017, 2018), a single-party regime has no margin for error; so, it is intrinsically linked with the expectations of the population, which, otherwise, with a strong repression, can be ignored, but, in that case, the regime won't be able to last for more than a few decades in the best-case scenario. It may seem paradoxical but easy to understand with a minimum of pragmatism. As a consequence the Chinese regime is wary of social discontent, and now China is the world leader in CO2 emissions as well as in energetic transition, and is the country of all records, the last of which being the building of the world's biggest floating solar energy plant with 166,000 photovoltaic panels on 800,000 square meters producing 40 megawatts since its entry into operational use in 2017. The revolution took place in transports too, with more and more electric vehicles and Tesla or Chinese charging points in all modern underground car parks. On a political level everything goes in the same direction: maybe it's a pose but it is China all the same, the country filled with contrasts, now becoming the green leader of the planet, particularly since Donald Trump have decided to withdraw from Paris treaties on climate (COP 21). Now, then, is China a polluted country? Yes, inevitably, one has never been able to make an omelette without breaking eggs. Is it beyond recovery? Of course not. Is the country doing enough to get out of it? It seems so. Will it be one of tomorrow's green countries? No one can tell, but it's giving itself the means to do so. May all the world quickly do the same, or we'll head for a disaster and no one will be able to blame China for it. Exporting air pollution to factory-countries is quite practical for our countries on the way of deindustrialisation, but we must keep in mind that we all live on the same planet.

4.   "CHINA IS A DICTATORSHIP"

We have already started treating this vast interesting subject before, in the chapter on pollution. Is China a dictatorship? It's certainly nearer to it than a rule of law system with many counter-powers, like most of the western democracies, some of which I prefer, by the way they operate and the absence of power concentration. Anyway, it doesn't meet the standards of western democracy, it's no use denying it. But an interesting fact is the third way opened by China: for the first time, a country, whose party in power is based on socialist ideology, uses the codes of the "market capitalism". It's a strange paradox, as plenty of other elements in China, but it looks as if it works well, up to now. Let's then come back to the fundamentals and we will perhaps be able to draw comparisons so as to rebalance criticisms, however legitimate they may be.

First of all, how does the Chinese political system work? This is really the first question to ask before stating what is repeated by people or groups (individuals, political parties, foreign leaders, associations) with a strong negative bias, trying to influence their audience as much as possible. That's valid for every subject: getting the habit of checking one's sources is recommended and should be generalized, especially now, when the phrase "fake news" is so often used. As on other topics concerning China, in the first rank, the best is always to discuss with the people (i.e. Chinese living in China) and carry out research from various sources, which I personally did several times. The Chinese Internet is limited or censored on subjects that the State considers as belonging to national security or the Party, but outside Internet contains a lot of information which the well-equipped Chinese can easily feed when they spend some time abroad.

To begin with, the fact China (the People's Republic of China) is a single-party regime is very important. The Chinese communist party (CCP) was founded in Shanghai in 1921 in a dim-looking building of the French Concession where only 13 delegates representing all the Chinese provinces had decided to meet. So it was founded in secrecy (the meeting was nearly interrupted by the French police): they wanted to defend a revolutionary movement for the young republic of China (after the fall of the last imperial dynasty, the Qing dynasty) to defend the model of international socialism to unite the country during that period of instability, a country devastated by warlords, under the growing influence of a nationalist Japan taking root on the continent. That young CCP even became the ally of Sun Yat-sen's republican party, the Kuomintang, till the end of the 1920s when Chiang-Kai-shek, the Kuomintang nationalist leader, after the country had been united under the republican banner, turned against the communists. As a consequence, it brought civil war in China (interrupted momentarily by the occupation of Japan) until Mao's CCP controlled the whole country in 1949 and proclaimed the People's Republic of China (with the exception of Taiwan where Chiang-Kai-shek's Republic of China had taken refuge).

Without going further into detail, which would be irrelevant, let's simply note that, since its foundation under the auspices of CCP, modern China has had a single party regime. The original constitution of the PRC gave a definition of the regime as being "a socialist State of popular democratic dictatorship, directed by the working-class and based on the alliance of workers and peasants". Quite a nice declaration, both obsolete and improper when we think of today's China, but such is the concept: a people's democratic dictatorship, based on the old socialist idea of the dictatorship of proletariat. So "popular" means "the people down below" with the withdrawal of prominent people (wealthy peasants owning lands, intellectuals, traders and capital holders…). Common points can be found with the soviet system and even with the French revolution in the sense that everyone must follow the direction of the revolution and its doctrine in which values, traditions and representatives of the old world have to retract or disappear. A kind of social upheaval made possible by the exasperation leading to revolutions. And, as in any revolution, it often leads to irreparable damage, even if we must confess that some great opportunities and benefits can result from the changes imposed at the cost of enormous sacrifices.

Since the time of Maoism and without questioning the role of the old leader (Mao is still considered as the father of the People's Republic and the leader of China's new emancipation), the party and, as a consequence, the country has progressed a lot, both socially and economically. The old socialist values of the beginning, defended by our fellows of 1968 in France at the end of the "great thirty years boom", have collapsed under unbridled capitalism. Yet, on a political plan, it's more or less the same, with the addition of a few reforms initiated by Deng Xiao Ping in the 1980s. Ideology always refers to Marxism, though, after the opening of the country, it has become a sort of "market socialism" (once more a Chinese exception). China is still controlled by the CCP at all levels of national, provincial and local government, which, we must admit it, is in the pure Chinese tradition, the CCP having taken the place of what existed in imperial China. Thousands of year habits die hard.

Today it is estimated that a little less than 100 million people are members of the CCP. Traditionally, it was necessary to be a member of the party to have some political, social or economic power and accession to the party could open many doors. Clarifying that question today isn't easy but it's highly probable that belonging to the party makes things easier in such a centralized and controlled political system. The new economic tycoons have fully understood and have worked with the party for long years now.

The Chinese power rests on three organs: the National Popular Assembly (3,000 deputies indirectly elected for 5 years having legislative power and controlled by CCP), the President (chief of the executive and armies and often party leader, appointed by the assembly following a personal recommendation of the party), and the Council for State Affairs (composed of ministers and administrative counsellors named by the President, chosen by the prime Minister and approved by the Assembly for a five year term, renewable once, [no longer true today since the Chinese executive reform], whose function is to elaborate and put into practice the government measures or suggest laws to the Assembly). The main decisions concerning the country are taken during the party congress, taking place every year with the 300 members of the central committee, who determine the political line of the whole country.

Though all the powers are exercised in separated organs, there's no clear separation as in the western democratic system, as the CCP is on top of the scaffold tower and inside it. In that sense, the regime could be considered as a dictatorship if the concentration of powers is the standard measure. But the notion of dictatorship is very vague. We must understand what we are talking about: if a dictatorship is a concentration of power in the hands of a minority, it's also the definition of aristocracy; if it is a power exerted by one man in the Roman way and then given back to the Senate, it doesn't look like the Chinese regime; if it's a word used to mention the fact that citizens don't vote, it's irrelevant as they can vote to choose their representatives. Locally there are popular assemblies that elect the popular assembly above them. Every five years, representatives of popular assemblies are directly elected; they govern locally, and they can stand for election as soon as they are supported by 10 citizens in their district. Nevertheless, as we can imagine, the CCP keeps under control those candidates who will elect other representatives, up to the members of the National Popular Assembly who will finally elect the President of the People's Republic.

So we can see that, in spite of elections, we can't consider China as a democracy. A democracy is a system where citizens can choose representatives who are not under influence or under the control of a third party. On this matter, by the way, what countries are really democratic (direct universal suffrage, absolute separation of powers, lack of pressure on candidates or conflicts of interest by means of corruption…)? It is difficult to say and a lot of our western contemporaries think so, as they feel they are not represented by their own institutions.

China at present is closer to dictatorship (even if it's different from all the characteristics of such a political system) than to democracy, notwithstanding elections. It's a special system accepted by a majority of people and adapted to the local mentality soaked with Confucianism, the respect of traditions and authority represented by the family (the elders) and the state power. Obviously, democracy is a western concept coming from ancient Greece (which, by the way, was equally unfair in many cases, with restricted rights to vote, women being put aside as well as the non-citizens named "Metics"). More recently in our country, less than a century ago, democratic regimes were very restrictive too. The right to vote was granted to women in France after 1944 though the country's political system was unquestionably considered as a model of development and freedom before.

Therefore, it's more reasonable to consider China as a hybrid system, far from democracy indeed, but it should not be easy for us to pass judgement. The important thing is that it works and is accepted by a majority of inhabitants, even if it can be difficult to praise an authoritarian regime. The beginnings were hard between 1949 and 1980. The country was poor, devastated by war, on the winning side after the last world conflict, but having endured pain and torment and being far from a great power status. The people had suffered, and the transition took place in pain because of the decisions taken by Party cadres and acknowledged today as mistakes (for example the Cultural Revolution) notably during trials covered by media concerning the "gang of four". With the alliance of economic market and socialism we are facing the paradox of a party in power that claims to be the party of workers and peasants but works as a capitalistic system. And it's incredibly effective: it enabled to get out of poverty hundreds of million people. Most of the members of the civil society were ignored but the results are there to see. The country's economic achievement, allowed by a strong State hand more authoritarian than in a democracy, has supported the party in the population's mind, as well as the prestige regained. Of course, there is some propaganda and the answers of the population, when questioned on various subjects, can sound as if they had been already told. There are also aspirations for more implication in political life as is demonstrated by the vigorous activity, often forbidden, of the Chinese blogosphere on the Internet. Besides, there is a real sincerity in the fact that many Chinese think their leaders are effective and they answer that the political system suits them. Let's not forget the words of Deng Xiao Ping, the father of China's opening to the world: "the colour of a cat, white or black, isn't important, what's important is that it catches the mouse". It's the result that counts, so what's important is to catch the mouse. And today the cat seems to be a good hunter.

Maybe all the people are not adapted to the western liberal democracy and the state of mind (typically in France we must admit) systematically criticizing and putting into question powers isn't so common in Asia and especially in China. Democracy isn't an Asian concept and, except maybe in Japan, is often distorted or perverted in its form (South Korea, South-East Asia). Many counties are prosperous in Asia in spite of their authoritarian regime: let's mention the convincing example of Singapore with a hybrid political regime where every aspect of society is strictly controlled by the State. People are not unhappy and often consider their state-city as an example, ignoring the political issues on the subject.

We must also take into account that the Chinese State doesn't strictly have the full powers. They have to take care of the population and unpopular measures can't be easily imposed. For example, they wanted to suppress the Hukou, a kind of passport linking every Chinese with his native region, used to stop movements of population and property speculation. It's a factor of stabilisation but it can be a handicap in some cases. They wanted to suppress it for Chinese living in foreign countries only, and for Shanghai in a first stage (a test period). Under several conditions, it might have finally ended in a withdrawal of nationality imposed on Chinese living abroad, as the Hukou is necessary to renew identity cards or passports and a lot of important juridical acts. In just a week, in front of a real social rebellion supported by websites, the proposal was withdrawn. Apparently, it didn't come straight from the top of the State but rather from too zealous secondary officials. This is a good illustration of the fact that, even in a regime considered as authoritarian by the western world, what is good for the people is also good for the party in power, which can lose a lot from instability. As we have been taught by revolutions, angry crowds can't always be mastered.

As a conclusion, I don't wish to take sides for a particular regime as it's not the aim of this book. Even if complete objectivity is impossible, I just hope that I'll make the reader realize that, on this subject, the rule of the double standard is too often used by people who are supposed to inform us. Unfortunately, the West too often tends to give lessons when our democracies more and more look like ochlocracies, i.e. the power of crowds, and are less and less representative of the republican and liberal ideal, with elections where the voting rate is lower and lower. Slowly but surely our societies become less free and less concerned by a true long term view and decision making of a well-informed public which is the basis of democracy: attacks by media, disinformation and "fake news", corruption of "elites" by various lobbies, public denunciation, people left to the mercy of social networks, lack of legitimacy of elections with a low voting rate and systematic disapproval of parliamentary laws by street demonstrations are a few examples of the present current excesses.

The word freedom has different meanings for a Frenchman and for a Chinese. A Frenchman thinks of political freedom, freedom of opinion and expression which indeed is more important in France than in China where a single party has power and controls public expression. On the contrary the Chinese think of the freedom of taking actions and making decisions in their daily lives. From this point of view, it seems to me that a Chinese has more freedom than a Frenchman who must respect more laws and rules, notwithstanding the global tax rate. Both of them keep their own views and seem to be glad about it. For instance, the Chinese do not understand why they should mock the President or the government all the time. For them it is just useless.

If the course followed by our democracies today isn't corrected, it will be interesting, in a few dozen years, to count points. Which of them will win the battle of ideas, the western democratic countries at present full of doubts, or their competitors in the developing world with highly regulated economies? The battle will probably be more economic than politic and, if we are not careful, the law of the strongest might determine the winner more easily than the ideas conceived in the age of Enlightment.

5. "CHINESE PEOPLE ONLY THINK OF MONEY"

The Chinese and Asian people, as a rule, are said to be too materialistic. They are supposed to be obsessed by money, work and the benefits that can be done, especially women, described as harpies of modern times, without any feelings, who only swear by jewels, high fashion clothes, sports cars, gourmet restaurants and luxury real estate. And they don't work, of course.

That distorted image now belongs to our collective psyche, but not for long, as 20 years ago the little Chinese were depicted as starving, to make our own children clean their plates. Today the little Africans play the same part to make our little ones feel guilty and eat up their broccoli.

The image of the Chinese obsessed by money may have been progressively created for two reasons. First, the Europeans and the French are now aware that not only Japanese but all Asian people are more well-to-do. A middle class has appeared with a better standard of living. Previously a wealthier upper class had made up, to which belonged political leaders and business managers after the economic liberalisation. Such an evolution has been observed more or less similarly in Korea and other "dragon" countries like Taiwan or Singapore, then in China and all East Asia in the years 1990-2000.

So Chinese people now travel and spend their money. The young Chinese study abroad with a significant budget for their accommodation and school fees. Slowly, since the beginning of the years 2000 (but the movement, which can no longer be ignored, has really amplified since the last ten years), the French are getting used to seeing Chinese tourists, wealthy or not, spending and spending on luxury goods in department stores. The phenomenon had grown to such an extent that, very quickly, all the stores had salespeople speaking Mandarin fluently on their booths. In Paris Galeries Lafayette ("lao fo ye" as Chinese people say) they have opened a special department devoted to Chinese consumers only with all commodities to take care of them and their wallets without disturbing others.

The second factor which, according to me, was at the origin of the belief that Chinese people only think of money is less visible and seems to be a kind of prejudice or, at least, a form of exaggeration concerning particular cases. A few years ago, the "marriage business" in China became an interesting subject for several western media. As a matter of fact, there are a lot of weddings in China, and a beautiful wedding is essential for a young couple who must respect the tradition to make their families happy and proud. But there's a rub: in China, owing to the birth limitation laws and the problem of abandoned children, there are fewer women than men, chiefly in rural areas. Indeed today the deficit is almost wiped off by measures taken (to know the sex of a child is forbidden before the foetus is several months old, couples with a single child are allowed to have a second one) but it has caused tensions during the last years. In a country where the capitalist system has been adopted, the rules of supply and demand prevail. So, there has been a lack of supply concerning women, I daresay, and a growing demand of men looking for a partner. As a result, women are rare. In some rich developed towns like

Shanghai, women have become much more demanding in front of men in despair of finding a life companion. Beyond a certain age too, the social pressure did the rest with sentences like "you should get married quickly or else, only bad matches will be left", "what will the neighbours and the family say?"…Then bids could start: to be "marriageable" a man should have a certain level of income and, with more tension, he should have his own vehicle to offer his wife maximum comfort. Then, in zones of real estate pressure like Shanghai or Beijing, with prices per square meter sometimes higher than in the best quarters of Paris, it became fashionable for a future husband to have his own flat and be physically attractive of course.

You understand my point: starting from particular cases which are far from being general, all the Chinese young girls were soon depicted as cupid, money being the only standard for a successful marriage.

Such a picture was conveyed by many reports on "husband markets" which western media broadcast with astonishment. Indeed, those places where parents come with their son's CV to answer the demands of free young (or not so much) women's parents, can strike the minds.

Yes, there are cupid people as elsewhere. I don't feel that the Chinese are more cupid than other peoples. However, they speak of money more freely than in other countries, and that difference is very important in France. Here we often consider money as something shameful (myth of the rich man enriching himself at the expense of the poor, or jealousy of people who have been less successful), but, in China and other Asian countries, it's quite different. This tendency is also less marked in Anglo-Saxon countries. Still we are far from the obsession of money criticized by some people. In China money has a social value first of all. Of course, money is used by individuals, but the link with money is much less individualistic than in the West. For example the Chinese are very generous with their families and their friends. There, meals are offered: a single person invites everybody. No complicated calculations, the other guests will have the opportunity to catch up or will offer something similar in value, a meal or a present. In China presents are regularly offered without any special occasion. You offer, then you receive. Presents and generosity are social markers which are also emphasized by Buddhist philosophy and Confucianism. Presents are a means to tighten the links, show one's affection and respect, give thanks or obtain favours. The face or "Mian Zi" is important and the presents received or offered are involved in it. It is the public image of someone which builds their reputation and social power. Money is just a means and rarely the objective. And, if in China people often ask the price of a present, you do not have to feel offended: it's just to know the value of it in order to be as generous to give back in return. Yes, there are stingy people and profiteers, but that state of mind is less common there, because of the strength of the "Mian Zi". The Chinese spending fortunes in French luxury stores, do you think it's for them? No, most of their purchases are presents for their families and friends, French luxury products being much less expensive in France than in China where freight charges and the trade margin greatly affect the price. Other acquaintances may have placed orders: in that case the Chinese travelling in Paris will buy for them and will be refunded the strict price of the goods. I give another personal example clearly showing the Chinese generosity: at my wedding, partly organized in France, there were about 50 French, family members or friends, and 15

Chinese, most of them close family members. Believe it or not, the contribution (without including our direct respective parents) paid for the wedding list by the Chinese was 2.5 times as high as what was paid by the French. That is a ratio of 8 to 1 per person. I fully understand that it's cultural, so making comparisons is inappropriate. But when we hear stories of people invited at a wedding without giving a present, it sounds totally inconceivable for a Chinese, at least for the Chinese I am lucky to go around with. Such an attitude would be a real insult for many Chinese, a friend being worth much more than some sparing of money.

In the bosom of the family, generosity is still more striking. Many French families are used to bequeathing their property to their children, sometimes making donations and giving presents, but their real estate and assets are separated as soon as the children come of age, and the latter have to be financially independent. They have been taught to manage alone, which can be a good thing but is sometimes too rigid, especially when the children live in places where the cost of living and real estate are expensive. In Chinese families, even if they also appreciate and encourage their children's financial independence, the progress is somewhat different. Parents often make important presents to their children, regularly and without any special reason, just to please them and help them save a little money when they need it, when they start out in life or have children, not at the time they will inherit. I could realize it with my Chinese family in law: now, while shopping, I avoid showing too much interest for any article, particularly when it's expensive, because if my mother-in-law notices it, she'll try to buy it for me, out of kindness, even if it's beyond her means. She can insist on paying for restaurant bills even if I want to pay for them. She would sacrifice her own expenses to pay for her children's. Once more that's cultural and I don't try to know which tradition is the best. However, China is exceptional in that respect: the Chinese are the only inhabitants in the world, to my knowledge, who can fight for paying a restaurant bill. I have seen people grasped by their friends to prevent them from paying the bill, while someone else was paying. For them money doesn't have to be accumulated for the sole purpose of it, as it should be used to buy an image, respect, favours or bring happiness to their close relations. By such examples I am trying to show that Chinese people are not at all obsessed by money itself. They spend it and, doing so, it gives them more satisfaction than accumulate it in a bank account. So we are far from the image of a moneygrubber and I have never been so warmly welcomed than in China where I could travel and enjoy great experiences without spending a yuan. It's not exceptional; it comes from the sense of hospitality depending on one's means, of course. We just have to understand the reason why they behave like that, which is not materialistic, and be able to be generous and hospitable too. They have no inferiority complex towards western countries, but just a tradition of hospitality and a true generosity we must be able to give back, when the opportunity arises. Kindness and hospitality are never lost: it could be the motto of the Chinese I have met.

6. "ALL THE CHINESE PEOPLE EAT STRANGE THINGS"

Let's review what the Chinese eat and what Chinese cuisine is. First, there are many different cuisines, Chinese cooking in general being called "zhongguo cai". We mustn't forget that the country is immense, as large as Europe. It's a continent with various climates, landscapes, inhabitants and, as a consequence, it gave birth to a great variety of cuisines and specialities. In France, generally, (and it seems to be the case in many western countries) we don't make the difference between Chinese and Vietnamese cuisines. Such a confusion probably comes from the time when Vietnamese and people from the ex-French colonial empire were in greater numbers in France than the Chinese. It was true until the 1980s. There is a lack of knowledge about Asia in general, with a constant confusion between Chinese, Japanese, Vietnamese, Koreans, Laotians, Cambodians and Thai people. For some of our country people they are all Chinese. So, Asian restaurants with specialities coming from different countries are called "Chinese" restaurants, where you can eat spring rolls which are more Vietnamese than Chinese. The local Chinese cuisine is unknown to a lot of us which is too bad, as it is rich, varied and has a long history.

In China, at least 8 main cuisines can be found: from Shandong, Jiangsu, Anhui, Zhejiang, Fujian, Guangdong, Hunan and Sichuan.

Reviewing them is worthy of interest. Shandong cuisine comes from a province near the east coast of China, south of Beijing. It's based on sea food and soups. Jiangsu cuisine, which I know best as it's near

Shanghai where my Chinese relations live, comes from a wealthy area around Shanghai up to Nanjing, the old capital ("Nan" meaning south and "Jing" meaning capital, the capital of the south, like Beijing "Bei Jing" is the capital of the north), with the lake district and Tai Hu big lake. Owing to a favourable climate and a fertile soil, it's a rich cuisine with sweet-flavoured vegetables, rice soups, tender meats and river food (fish, shrimps, crabs and ducks). "Xiao Long Bao" is an excellent speciality of steam-cooked patties stuffed with meat in a delicious broth. The best ones are cooked in Suzhou, near Shanghai, and despite my efforts, I have never found the same flavour in western countries.

Anhui cuisine comes from a region east of China, above Jiangsu, around the basin of the best-known Chinese river, Yangzi Jiang (the Yangtze). With mountains and plains, it's a mixed cuisine of game and sea food too, with hotpots (Huo Guo), fish or meat dishes, spicy or with aromatic herbs.

Then, Zhejiang (south of Shanghai, with Hangzhou, the biggest city in the province) has a cuisine with poultry, fish and other sea food, bamboo shoots, Huang Jiu (yellow wine) and tea quite famous there.

Fujian (southeast coast of China) produces sea food, rice, soups in the sweet-sour, steam-cooked or fried style.

Guangdong is the region of Guangzhou in the south. Their cuisine is well-known and very important for the inhabitants and all sorts of food can be eaten there. It's probably the only Chinese cooking with such a variety of products and some of them can seem strange to non-Chinese as well as to Chinese people themselves. Insects, snakes, bush meat are to be found on menus with offal or other parts which nobody, except in that province, is used to eating. A popular saying claims that Guangzhou people "eat all four-legged things except tables and chairs". Local cuisine is an institution there, but it doesn't mean that all the Chinese like it, because they can find in it specialities too strange for their personal taste. It's just like some specialities of Lyons cuisine (France), famous all over the world, with dishes containing offal, which many people don't want to eat. Other food preparations of the region of Guangzhou are highly appreciated in the West, for instance sweet-sour pork or with caramel sauce.

Hunan cuisine can be tasted too, with stews, fried dishes, smoked products and red pepper.

Finally we can mention the cuisine of Sichuan, a mountainous province (capital: Chengdu) near Tibet specialized in delicious dishes made of beef, spices, Sichuan pepper with its special flavour, and hotpots (a spicy broth in which the guests cook all sorts of ingredients, turning the meal into a festive party still more friendly than a traditional Chinese meal which, in essence, is already very lively).

As a conclusion, we could also mention the Yunnan cuisine (south China near Vietnam) with very spicy and more "tropical" dishes and where high-quality teas are produced.

After a review which may seem a bit too long (thank you for your patience), we haven't said anything to do justice to the Chinese cuisine, which shows how varied it can be, and which can't be limited to spring rolls eaten in a western fast-food Asian restaurant.

Among hundreds of cooking specialities there are obviously some which don't suit western tastes or make a mark on minds. I have personally tasted several of them and they are not so terrible that their names might suggest. Nevertheless, it's necessary to defuse controversy concerning dog meat: 99% of the Chinese don't eat it and are indifferent or find it revolting and archaic. The tradition is still alive, almost exclusively, in one town (Yulin) after the end of similar festivals turned towards dog meat in other provinces (festivals where a lot of dogs were consumed, special dogs raised for their meat, not poodles or pet dogs taken away from their families of course). Nowadays associations dedicated to animal welfare are working for a total ban of Yulin festival and its existence appears to be more and more compromised. Whatever our opinion on the subject may be, (especially concerning the methods of slaughter considered as barbaric) we must note that the central point of debate is our perception of animals: are dogs more sacred than cows? Is it because they are closer to us and more intelligent? Cows are sensitive animals too. In India, eating cows isn't tolerable for a lot of people whereas in France we do it, with sometimes quite abominable slaughter methods. We also eat octopuses, which are very clever. Many animals consumed as human food are presented as less intelligent than they are, not to shock populations. So we can say that cultural differences justify taboos on certain foods, but, for a true defender of animals, all of them should be considered as sensitive creatures, and treating them equally with a minimum of stress and suffering is more important than cultural attacks, all the more so as Korea and other Asian countries eat more dogs than China, in general indifference. China is the focus of all the attacks when, all over the country, fewer and fewer people support those practices.

Let's now review the dishes that seem strange according to western tastes. Here I will only talk about what I know:

- Jellyfish: it can really be considered as disgusting. However, it's edible! Of course, they are not to be eaten gluey but cooked with a special seasoning and served in salads with other ingredients like raw vegetable hors d'oeuvres. When well prepared, they taste like black Asian mushrooms, not very tasty and a little crispy; they are quite tolerable for my taste with a suitable sauce. Consumed alone they are much less pleasant.

- Sea cucumbers: considered as disgusting by excellence, it's in fact very good when well prepared. It's different from the sort we can find in the seas of Europe, which is too big with a thick skin. In good restaurants small sea cucumbers are perfectly emptied and cooked. The bowels inside are not edible. Outside the skin makes up a sort of pancake, stuffed with various fillings and served in a broth. Those culinary specialities are usually very expensive as they are quite rare and need a lot of preparation; they were offered to me several times and I found them excellent: they are dainty dishes chosen to honour one's guest.

- Edible bird's nests: a dish highly caricatured as it's not the bird's real nest made of mud, twigs and saliva. Clearly what the European folklore says is false, such nests are not consumed. Only a special kind of swallow (in fact a swift) builds an edible nest made with the mucus secreted by the bird. Those nests are washed, and they are then similar to small translucent heaps looking like dried noodles stuck together. The fibres can be added to dishes consumed in China or other far-eastern countries such as Thailand.

- Sharks: shark fins are always well-prepared in good restaurants. It's a very expensive tasty speciality. But I think it should be better to limit or to ban its consumption as the number of sharks in the oceans is dramatically falling. Movies like "Jaws" have had a very bad impact on sharks, despised by the general public, when they are very useful and can be considered as the cleaners of the seas. So, in spite of its fine taste and touch of prestige, such a dish should no longer be offered and marketed. I have tasted it twice, as a guest in a Beijing restaurant, it was indeed excellent, but I am not proud of having contributed to its trade.

- Fugu or balloon-fish: maybe the least strange among those specialities, it's that famous fish bristling with pikes which can inflate itself like a balloon to be protected from predators (which, too bad for it, is ineffective with fishermen). Cooks need a special rigorous training to avoid a deadly toxin if the fish isn't prepared correctly. It's commonly consumed in Japan as well as in China, where it is cooked and its skin is eaten all at once, causing a sort of scratchy feeling when it goes down into the oesophagus. It's tasty because of the special preparation, but I found its flesh rather common.

- Pig skins: such a name isn't very enticing. It's a dish made with small pieces of pork and the skin (lower layer) and fat under the skin. As it contains a lot of collagen it's considered as a "medicine" dish. As a matter of fact, in China, people eat for health care and pay attention to the peculiar qualities of dishes. I don't like fat, but I confess that dish can be easily consumed with a good sauce. It's not more shocking than other pork specialities we can find in Europe, like the pig ears consumed in Portugal for example.

- Chicken feet: it's a dish I am far from being crazy about, but all tastes are in nature. They can be even sold in little bags and people eat them as spicy condiments or as ingredients in more elaborate dishes. Many Chinese are fond of them and so are a few French, but I am afraid I'll never be able to cross that cultural gap.

- Cow's stomachs: cut in small pieces, it's used in hotpots. I am not particularly keen on it but it's edible.

- Turtles: in some restaurants you can see them in aquariums and customers can choose them, exactly as in France with lobsters or crabs. It is river turtles, to be precise. I have never felt like eating those animals. In the province of Guangdong, they eat snakes too and people say they taste like chicken.

Apart from those typical dishes I have never seen incredible or really disgusting things like scorpions or insects, often presented as some market folklore.

Now then, in Chinese cuisine there are "strange" specialities for inexperienced taste buds, but an open-minded westerner can perfectly consume more than 90% of local dishes. Trying to taste a maximum of dishes is a good attitude, and I do my best when I am invited in a local restaurant. The Chinese are very happy when we are interested in their culture and the first step is to taste their cooking. The French can easily understand it, as they are close to the Chinese who enjoy the pleasure of food like them. Chinese people really appreciate when foreigners taste their cuisine, thank them a lot and say what they think of it (without offending them by gratuitous criticism). We don't have to like everything, and they don't either, when they are abroad. They will perfectly understand that some dishes are unusual and different from our culinary habits. It's not surprising that some dishes are more difficult to eat or imagine for people coming from abroad, all the more so as that cuisine is rich with thousands of different dishes. The products are not the same as in Europe, with an unequalled variety of vegetables for instance. So I don't think the Chinese cuisine is so strange. On the contrary it's enriched by those differences. With the French, Italian and Japanese cuisines, it's probably the most varied and elaborate in the world. It has been created and improved for centuries and it belongs to the intangible heritage of humanity.

7. "CHINESE PEOPLE ARE COMMUNISTS"

Are the Chinese communists? (a question which has already been mentioned in a previous chapter on "dictatorship"). No, they are not. All the Germans were not Nazis, all the Russians were not Bolsheviks and all the French were not collaborators or members of the resistance movement between 1940-1944, so, similarly, the Chinese population is not communist. Only some members of civil society holding major positions in their fields can belong to CCP, but their importance is rather secondary and they are light years away far from Marxist ideology; at least nowadays for most of them. Belonging to the Party is more utilitarian than strategic for both sides: a membership card can be a lever for higher social standing and the CCP can control economic decisions more easily.

On the contrary I think that the population isn't interested in this question. According to my perception and after listening to many discussions on this topic, there are two major groups in the population: the people who have known China before the economic, politic and moral liberalization (i.e. the generation before Deng Xiaoping and the great changes in the 1980s) and the younger generations who are twenty or thirty year old, who were born after 1980 and 1990.

The older generation has known the time of propaganda and upheavals when the CCP progressively took control of the country. Some of them have known the war, the indirect confrontation with the western block during the cold war, as well as hardship and chaos in some parts of China in the years 1940-50-60. They suffered famines too, caused by risky decisions taken by the communist leaders such as the great leap forward and the Cultural Revolution, but also by the rapidly-increasing population. That difficult period of hardship and suffering, linked with strong ideologist propaganda, has made that generation immune to policy, as they had to adapt themselves to the situation without being involved in the decision-making process. Paradoxically that old generation sees the regime as a saviour. At the end of the war, the Kuomintang, Chiang Kai-shek's nationalist party wasn't welcomed: it was criticized for its lack of reaction or spirit of resistance against the Japanese invaders (right or wrong, because of collaborationists in its ranks). We must admit that the Japanese regime has committed massacres and abuses in the country, which is very little mentioned in Europe (massacres of Nanjing still denied to day by some politicians in Japan, estimated 200,000 to 300,000 deaths). That's also why the CCP won the civil war: the population of peasants supported Mao's communists because they considered them as real resistance fighters as they didn't lose hope and remained active during the dark hours of occupation. A Chinese proverb says that a sparkle is enough to give birth to a big fire: after the long march, the communists were almost reduced to nothing, but they could rally a part of the population to their cause by their speeches about peasants (in a mostly rural country) and their fighting spirit against invaders, which, at the time, had a strong impact in the rural areas suffering from the abuses of the Japanese occupation. Moreover, later they were considered as a means for the country to free themselves from successive dominations (of Europe for more than a century, then of Japan for a few decades). I think it was a way to cut the links. Today that generation of old Chinese is almost completely depoliticized and doesn't criticize the leadership of China. They are greatly confident in the leaders of the country and they value their community first, for which they have accepted to make sacrifices, considered as positive for the common good, even if that feeling isn't always fully justified. The conditions of life have greatly improved in the last 60 or 70 years, so that generation isn't critical about China's political line these last 40 years, and criticisms concerning the regime are never expressed, with the exception of some personal cases.

The second group, made up with the young generations, has never known the hard times of the past, more or less caused by the decisions of the CCP. They have been the witnesses of China's revival with its economic liberation and the gigantic growth of the country in 40 years. Today's world and the world when they were born have nothing in common: the landscape has changed with urbanization, and so has the structure of cities, like the way of life in a society gradually moving towards a connected economy, going from heavy industry to innovation, like other Asian countries (South Korea for instance). They have always known the communist regime and didn't suffer from it. Stability is a must for them. My point of view may be a little distorted as I didn't meet the expectations of people living in rural areas, but that young generation is generally quite moderate (except some more radical groups, independent or more or less influenced by lobbies, without much impact on public opinion). That young generation often thinks of what is good for the whole country, despite a growing individualism which is still far from the level observed in our more permissive countries. It's a generation more politically involved than their elders, but not revolutionary. They are against the idea of causing troubles to get more democracy and consider that disturbances would be a danger for the economy and the country. They have travelled abroad; they are educated and have often studied in foreign countries or have met foreign students in China; they are pragmatic and know their history. They refuse chaos and know the limitations of China where priority was to feed the population, a difficult task in a country with 20% of the world population and 10% of cultivable land. They are also aware of the difficulties to govern a country with 1.4 billion inhabitants whose standards of living, culture and education are still so different. On that subject, they often compare China with its rival, India, where they consider that the democratic system, with its permissiveness, is responsible of the lack of development and concrete progress. So that generation of 20-30-year-old people believes that some moderation is necessary to reform the country politically and progressively. They also think that western countries are not always their friends and consider that the frequent admonitions of the defenders of democracy are attempts to weaken China by imposing internal troubles ending with a general chaos. They also know that, in western countries, democracy often appeared after the economic development and industrial revolutions. So they are patient and their priority is a better life. That said, it doesn't prevent them from regretting the absence of debate and the frequent hardening of the regime on its political attributes. Their opinions are divided concerning the new directions of the CCP, in particular the lifting of the two-term presidential limit for the president Xi Jinping (a necessity to reform China in depth for some, but for others a drift towards totalitarianism), they would like to be allowed to discuss it more freely and without censorship, but are aware of the underlying risk that too much permissiveness could lead to social troubles. So they prefer to be confident in their government and support it, hoping to solve the problems at the proper time, the political problem being the last priority.

So that generation isn't communist. As said earlier, the regime is now far from the Marxist ideals, even if it claims it still refers to them. It is impossible to speak of communism in China today: the country is governed by a quasi-single party (there are groups and currents inside the party and other minor affiliated parties), with a capitalist market economy controlled by the State whose population is not at all socialist. With the exception of some idealists of the years 1950 to 1970 whose enthusiasm was cooled by market economy, it's difficult to find a real Marxist today in China. On the contrary in France we still have some, proclaimed or disguised under various labels of new left-wingers or revolutionaries, or supporters of ecology. You can find the same in the U.K. and even some of them are now visible in the U.S. Now then, how is it possible to say that China is so communist a country?

It could make us smile. To be convinced of it, you just have to walk in Shanghai or Beijing, where cash is king, and merchandising is everywhere, even in taxis with advertising screens bombarding you on the back of the car. Huge malls where you can spend whole days, food galore, money flowing, spent by "second generation" wealthy people you can see in the streets or in select clubs without taking any account of the government's warnings, property prices reaching a stratospheric level in some districts, payment facilities of all kinds (incorporated into mobile terminals without contact, facilitated fund transfers, facial-recognition payment devices), technological innovations and financial products facilitated by the abundance of domestic funds, the emergence of national champions specialized in information technologies, mobility (electric vehicles), aerospace industry, banks….But everything is controlled by the State's watchful eye through a titanic system discarding all inappropriate information. Capitals are controlled to ensure financial stability, which is quite annoying for some Chinese exposed to foreign investments, but is understandable as the government ensures stability. To conclude, I think it would be interesting to review the positive and negative aspects of the CCP power, a difficult and daring task, which won't enjoy unanimity, but it's interesting to take the risk.

To speak of the positive aspects of communism (or rather the system created by the CCP), it's difficult for me to find them in the communist doctrine (based on Marx's work), which brought very little to the country because I think it's both an utopia and a dangerous ideology denying any individuality which is the engine of human progress. However, the communists and Mao gave independence to China. After following the Soviet Union (who helped them during the civil war), they quickly separated because of growing disagreements and made their own way. So China became the leader of non-aligned countries in the world, which shaped its future. The country could remain united and keep or recover historical territories of ancient dynasties like Tibet or Inner Mongolia. If the Kuomintang had won, we can imagine they would have aligned themselves on the USA. Even if it wasn't a democracy (it disappeared very quickly after the advent of the Republic, when Chiang Kai-shek replaced Sun Yatsen), the Kuomintang regime would have been more liberal and more permissive. I think that whole territories would have left the Republic of China which would have lost Inner Mongolia, Xinjiang, and, of course, Tibet that would be today a sort of Nepal hardly developed, enclosed, feudal but independent. The independence and unification of China seem to be the result of Mao's party's action at the time, as well as modernisation. It was decided by the leader of the communist party with the opening of the country at the end of the 1970s: I refer to Deng Xiaoping whom I consider as a great strategist and pragmatic man. Though I am convinced that Deng Xiaoping wasn't a Marxist and proved it by his rational actions not depending on ideology, he remained a leader of CCP and his achievements must be credited to the party which benefited from it and was able to carry out his reforms.

Lastly, the third positive view engendered by the CCP was central planning and dirigisme. Some political decisions were serious mistakes and, as an aggravating factor, were made quickly without safeguards. Some others, like the single-child policy or modernisation projects and acquiring nuclear arms were crucial for the country. An authoritarian regime can benefit from a simplified and quick decision-making process. Objectively, it can be an advantage, and that's true for all authoritarian regimes, Marxist or not. Similarly, the fifth Republic of General de Gaulle in France can be considered as centrally-planned too; it was a democracy with a leader who could make independent decisions (to develop the atom bomb for instance) even when they were criticized by the international community.

Now let's speak of the multiple disadvantages of the communist regime: it's a grey view of reality (which is neither all black nor all white), I am trying to depict in this book. Let's mention three of them. First, of course, we mustn't forget the human tragedy. That revolution, supported by peasants with little or no education at all, has caused real social upheavals. To impose their views and strengthen the power of their party, the communist leaders have made lots of human victims and have created considerable delays: as a consequence of a reversed logic, peasants made decisions and intellectuals ploughed the fields. Luckily, they didn't continue the experiment, nevertheless it was dramatic for many citizens. Considering the lack of efficiency of such a policy, the only profit for Mao and his party was a stronger power. The losers were China and its inhabitants.

Secondly, the advent of communism disturbed the ancient Chinese society. Much of its patrimony was lost because it was considered as useless by the communist ideology to build a new kind of modern humanity liberated from any impediments. Good manners have declined, and a real culture has disappeared: the culture of ancient imperial China and Confucianism. Today it's coming to life again, but the damage is considerable, and this probably accounts for a lack of education among some Chinese people (observed severely by foreigners). An important architectural patrimony was unfortunately lost too.

Finally, a third point is the lack of transparency and individual freedom. The situation has improved but the system created by a single party in power has given birth to corruption. Today the President is always tackling the problem as it is a danger for the party legitimacy. With the rule of law, the reign of corruption is more difficult than in an opaque regime with few counter powers, which makes it still more punitive.

8. "CHINA WILL FOLLOW A PATH TOWARDS A MORE LIBERAL SOCIETY"

That's a common belief now rather out of date. It's heard less and less frequently, which shows that foreigners are getting used to the Chinese model. But we really can't be sure, and no one can predict the future. An evolution towards more democracy may appear, but today it looks as if the opposite is happening. We are in front of a unique political system which has developed by its own. Between 1949 and the beginning of the 2000s, China didn't actually stir up passions. It was considered as a backward country, not very interesting in the world's affairs. Maybe that's why it was left alone, and China could ensure its growth for two decades. Today it's become the heart of the global political strategy led by other countries (I mean world powers, the first of them being the USA). It's clear that Chinese people have made a lot of sacrifices and now want to gather the fruit from them, without any aggressiveness or any complex.

That depends of young people, who are wise enough: in spite of the existing problems, they can see the progress made, and try to favour stability and social success for the benefit of their families. The population harvesting the fruit of China's liberal policy loathes instability. As a consequence, young people can often be favourable to government measures. They nevertheless remain critical towards policy, though their criticisms are censored a lot. The situation doesn't move because they have no claims. But the young people belonging to the ethnic Chinese, studying and working abroad (with or without a

Chinese passport) have a different attitude. They tend to strengthen the image of a strong country because they benefit from it. Let's put things in perspective: in the twentieth century, the Chinese were seen as low-condition workers, political refugees, sometimes despised and considered as inferior to the local population of the countries where they lived. For example, in today's France, Chinese people, even when they speak a good French, find it difficult to integrate in the host country and suffer from a bad image in spite of the friendliness cultivated towards Asian people (compared with other foreign populations) because they are considered as discreet efficient workers. When they don't speak French, they stay among their fellows to help each other. To be more respected by westerners, the rank of China is important for them. The stronger and more respected their country, the more positive the effect on their condition. The nationals of major countries often have fewer problems and suffer less from prejudices and discriminations. So, though they know the political system and the liberal thought of the west, they will defend China and its policy and will sometimes hide its negative aspects from their own fellow countrymen, still living in their home country, via social networks, giving them lessons of tolerance and patriotism by comparing the situation of China with the difficulties that western democracies may encounter.

So the situation is extremely complex (a typical characteristic of China), with ambivalent signals concerning the perception of today's political regime by the young and old generations, the developed regions and others more remote, the Chinese living in China and those living abroad.

In which direction will China choose to go? Towards more democracy or a hard-line regime? Towards stability like today? Towards more tightened links with the west or, on the contrary, the affirmation of Chinese specificities?

Recent political decisions are deeply analysed, especially the suspension of the number of terms for the Chinese president who, now, can renew it as many times he likes. But can Xi really choose? His history is interesting. His father was a victim of the 1960s purges and yet Xi belongs to the CCP and defends its options. Today he isn't totally free, owing to the political and social situation of China. The old generations educated by the party are on the decline. They are not politically involved and never criticize the decisions of their leaders. They have grown in the 1960 and 1970 decades and tell their own children that they have been "raised by the party" and ask them not to be derogatory towards their leaders. On the other hand, the new generations, born after 1980-1990 and still more in the following years, tend to make a laughingstock of the political situation. They know the limitations of individual freedom but don't mind a lot as they prefer stability and pay more attention to their economic future and their children's, as noted earlier. And, as indicated previously, they can express criticisms under cover or openly, sometimes actively. So, for political leaders, the equation is becoming difficult. Progressive ideas or, at least, a will to question the legitimacy of the government and its practices are progressively taking place with the new generations. To ensure stability the state must react by giving a new layer of patriotism and original ideas from the party (authority, liberation, brotherhood, defence of peasants and workers). Such is the meaning of the reinforcement, by President Xi, of the state power on a patriotic base with a stronger control (at least more than in the years 2000s) of the liberty of expression. Some ideas are seen as threats for the power and have no voice at all.

For me, Xi is playing the part of a tightrope walker: on one hand, he is defending and promoting a party which hurt his family and whose errors, committed in the past, he is perfectly aware of (which will never be confessed publicly, not to weaken the party authority and favour the partisans of political destabilization). But on the other hand, he is strengthening his power, probably (that's my deep conviction) to reinforce the place of China in the world, its economy and independence, and to achieve it, stability is a must. His attitude is both firm and non-aggressive. He belongs to the new world order and uses its norms (member of the WTO, defender of free-trade, efforts towards a green economy via China's recent strategy to reduce pollution). Moreover Xi's fight against corruption is his spearhead action: it was a real plague in China; now it's less important but still exists. A peak was reached at the end of Hu Jintao's term and scandals were revealed in 2008 during the earthquake in Sichuan when in some places 99% of the Chinese donations for the victims were intercepted by great or small local leaders. This strategy is well regarded by the opinion which can't bear scandals discrediting the political world, but it has also created enemies; a lot of politicians, of all levels, have been condemned, as part of Xi's strategy attacking "the flies as well as the tigers", from small local mayors to great province leaders. If Xi leaves power now, when the job isn't done, his attempt will have been useless and corruption will flourish again, without forgetting the fact that harm might befall him from some groups seeking revenge. These points are for me logical reasons to keep power a little longer, the time for the situation to be stabilized.

My analysis is a personal one: Xi's hands are tied. He is the leader of China, he can be threatened if he leaves power, and he sees that the situation is dangerous for the unity of the country and its future success. According to me, his "no limit" term sets an example of sacrifice to try to secure China's future without destroying all the work done for so many years. Of course, I may be wrong, but I think many Chinese agree and share my point of view. The party still has a chance to modernize and bring satisfaction to a majority of people.

We mustn't forget that has been traumatized by what happened in the 19th and 20th centuries: independence from external powers is crucial. The country will never take the risk of reviving the past of humiliation, domination and massacres. The Chinese want to freely choose their destiny and a strong regime is the best they have found to make their yearning come true.

But the ending remains uncertain. If I have rightly guessed President Xi's conviction, the time will come when a new liberalization will be necessary. The fact of giving a strong country (with a president who can be elected for life) to anyone after that might be a disaster. And opposing the will of Chinese people, who are not against their institutions and leaders but will finally be against too much authority, is equally dangerous, as it might lead to a political situation out of control: it might give birth to excesses and a real internal confrontation destroying the work done by the people's sacrifices, for so many years, to rebuild the country.

Once more, China has very specific features. Nobody knows which way the country is going to choose, and I don't claim I am able to imagine or recommend one. No one can predict the future and as History often showed it, I know that the road to hell is paved with good intentions. The Chinese are free to do as they like, it's their choice: they can support their leaders or not, knowing that the strongest coercions can't prevent people from living according to their desires and from choosing their way sooner or later. So if the regime doesn't progress towards more "democracy", as we understand in the west (and apparently it doesn't look like it), it will be the sign of a different Chinese system and we'll need the courage to admit that the major part of the population is content with that state of things and their leaders' management. Despite the negative aspects, mentioned before, many of them being the consequence of the local constraints which no political regime could perfectly solve, a majority of Chinese are confident in Xi Jinping's decisions. The Chinese government doesn't trust western democracies and believes they are parentheses in history, whose democratic ideals are depraved by a dominating class looking like a new aristocracy. For China, the prosperous era of the Middle Kingdom is reflected by the Emperors, not by the Republic. Whatever name is used, communism, single party, Chinese capitalism, autocratic dirigisme, the result is the same: it looks as if we are witnessing the rebirth of the ancient Chinese order, i.e. a regime more or less centralised and authoritarian. Whatever the future may be, it would be wise to no longer confound Chinese regime with "communism", in spite of its official name and the history of the party, which is today the tool of Chinese renewal. As for the future, nobody can predict it but I am ready to bet that China won't be authoritarian like ancient Russia, or liberal like western countries, and will go on building its own model, as long as it will be able to meet the aspirations of its population. Don't let us forget that the history of China is original: without democracy the people has often overthrown political regimes out of real dissatisfaction. What is interesting now is that sort of fight we can watch between two blocks, two worlds: on one side western democracies and on the other less democratic regimes, more authoritarian, but apparently working, which our ideologists can hardly explain.

Who will win the ideological battle? A non-democratic system, which is apparently working, regulating its economy and making decisions quickly in spite of all the conflicts of interest at its head and all the possible abuse of power? Or the democracies slowly forgetting the reasons why they were founded, the principles of liberty, equality and the government of the people by the people? The difference which could tip the scale is probably the incitements between the people and the elite to look in the same direction. Despite the repression, above a certain level of dissatisfaction, the elite and the political system will fall in a spiral of violence, which both China and France have known during their respective revolutions of 1949 and 1789. Thereby, the Chinese system is strongly incited to do the right choices if the party wants to keep power. On the opposite, and it's a concern for us, it looks as if, in our democracies, more and more people, whose aspirations are neglected (except during election periods), become indifferent. The population refusing to vote or voting very little is considered as negligible. It's a corruption of democracy and its primary ideals as well as its operating mode. The elite more and more depends on lobbies and are tempted to act according to their views, which is a real conflict of interest with their electoral mandate. It's particularly true concerning the results of the American Presidential elections in 2016, where the popular movement (changing by definition) was influenced by inaccurate positions, not to say wrong (see the fake news scandal and foreign interference via the case Facebook/Cambridge Analytica) and where the democrat candidate was the winner by the number of ballot papers (it's a consequence of the American system with the Electoral College). The result of the election gave birth to a government which, in spite of the announcements made, is far from the preoccupations of dissatisfied or disadvantaged Americans who had brought it to power. The gap between the acts of the leaders and the demands of the population, which is more to be found in France and in Europe, is weakening our political systems which, through governments considered as democratic but unable to work, might lead to authoritarianism. The admiration for political systems appreciating "strong men", like Vladimir Putin's Russia, reveals the evolution of a growing part of the population in the West, and might change the face of our democracies before the end of the century. Maybe that's the new world order: a political decline favoured by a democratic regression in front of economic necessity.

Add-on in December 2019 about the Hong-Kong events

First of all, I must say that I know more Continental China that Hong Kong. Despite having friends and relations who have lived in Hong Kong for several years, or still live there, I have visited the Hong Kong SAR (Special Administrative Region) only three times. The second time was in late 2017 and the third time in late 2019 so there is a short comparison basis between both visits.

My understanding of the social unrest there, that has marked the year 2019 and is not resolved yet, is firstly that the situation is a lot more complex that it seems.

We see in the media some chocking scenes, such as Molotov cocktails and policemen on fire, or anti-riot forces charging protesters or even firing at them because they were beaten up with metal bars. We have seen roads blocked, Chinese banks burning, protest at Hong Kong airport. But it did not affect all the territory. As for the 'gilets jaunes' events in France (I have witnessed all of it), the media often exaggerates these situations, but not specifically on purpose, just because when you see images of civil war on TV you easily assume it is more violent that it is really on the field.

I have noticed that the media like to use the expression 'former British colony' for Hong Kong, and that they easily give voice to the protesters (who are sometimes rioters rather than protesters), and less easily to the Hong Kong government. They also frequently underline a 'fight for more democracy' without reminding us that the retrocession of Hong Kong from the UK administration to China in 1997 mentions that the "one country two systems" will apply only for 50 years, i.e. until 2047. At this date, Hong Kong will have the same laws as mainland China. Hong Kong is thus truly a part of China.

To my understanding, these riots are, like the vast majority of social unrest in the world during the last few years, a consequence of social difficulties of the younger population. It is easy to accuse China of all the problems, and it's true that the governance will also change and that Hong Kong citizens were used to more liberal views, but let's not forget that Hong Kong also has its own problems.

First, the SAR is no longer the only financial center in China as it suffers by more and more competition from Shanghai in continental China, and even from Shenzhen just a few kilometres away of the limits of Hong Kong. This will progressively decrease the importance of Hong Kong as a financial hub even if the city is still a link between East and West.

Second, Hong Kong is also, little by little, caught up by Guangzhou and other Chinese metropolitan areas in terms of standard of living. So the "frontier" between Hong Kong and the rest of China is less and less visible and the differences are slowly disappearing.

Third, the new economy is booming in China and cities such as Shenzhen, or Hangzhou are on the cutting edge on this field, with lots of start-ups, AI companies, etc. This is a field in which Hong Kong has no real advance so on that sector too the city has found new competition. The world around Hong Kong has changed faster than expected.

Last, and not least, the cost of living in Hong Kong becomes incredibly high, especially for real estate. The cost of housing can easily be out of proportion with income of new generations who just entered the labour market. Not to mention that large parts of the economy (real estate but also electricity, energy and so on) are locked up by big conglomerates owned by tycoons, which is not helping as prices remain high. If you have a lof of money, you can live extremely well in Hong Kong, but if you don't have this chance, the life is more difficult now than ever before.

In such a context, anyone can understand that a part of young population is angry and sees little improvement for their future, at least economically. And it is also easy, in such a context, to blame someone: China. In the UK or France, we blame the immigrants, in the US it's the liberals or the Mexican or China, in Africa it's Europe and colonization…everyone has its own devil.

It is also said that riots are fuelled by the West, or that people (locals or Chinese citizens living there) are even paid to participate in demonstrations. This is a fact closely watched by the Hong Kong and Chinese governments, but we will not make any further comment on this much sensible topic.

As far as I'm concerned, I had been warned about the fact it was not recommended to speak Mandarin now in Hong Kong (instead of Cantonese), as some continental Chinese have been beaten up in the street or were not served in restaurants or shops because of their origin. It is a sad thing if true, especially as the Hong Kong economy now relies more on more on continental Chinese consumption in the territory, like some parts of Japan or Korea. But when I went again to Hong Kong, I did not notice anything in particular except some graffiti in some parts of the city against the government. I (and the Chinese people with me as well) was warmly welcomed as usual, the city is still bustling, business as usual, and the people are still the same, as kind as they can be. I did not feel real animosity towards continental Chinese people, and I had the feeling of being in the same country as when I am in Shanghai (or say, Guangzhou because of the language). 1 country – 2 systems really. I hope this unity will not be broken in the future and that both parties are able to cooperate fully for the better good of all.

9. "THE CHINESE ARE TRYING TO CONQUER THE WORLD"

It's the topic of the day. Like other assertions making up the chapters of this book, it's a sentence we can often read or hear again for a few months, since Xi Jinping can, with the parliament's approval, serve more than two terms at the head of the country, which opens the way to terms renewed as many times as necessary. Everyone can understand that President Xi is undeniably the strong man of China, but what is more difficult to make out is the direction he wants to give to the Middle Kingdom. As stated before, we can imagine that the licence given to him will allow him to have time and flexibility to achieve the country's great plan: to be independent from western powers, first of all the USA, to get a status of regional or even worldwide power, in its zone of influence of the Pacific ocean and the South China sea, where the American armed forces are still present, and secure China's economic landing (which will need tact and reforms considering the weight of debts in the country's economy) and a restructuring of the creation of wealth (transition from an industrial GDP turned towards exportation to domestic consumption with the development of services and innovation).

Does China really want to build an empire? Is it a threat for its neighbours and the world? Does the world have to tremble, now that China is awake, as foretold by Alain Peyrefitte who knew the huge potential of the country and had worthily questioned the future of the world as soon as 1973, putting into perspective modern and ancient China?

I am tempted to give a negative answer to these questions, and I'll try to say why I am not particularly concerned. Or rather, I could be worried about the global evolution of the world, not only of China, because, with contemporary globalization, more than during the second world war, all the economies and countries are closely interlinked and can't free themselves from the strategies, reactions and consequences of their neighbours' actions.

Why am I not so much concerned? The first reason is historical. People say history tends to repeat itself: concerning China, throughout the ages, we can't say it's a country trying to get involved beyond its borders or its protectorates. China has always given priority to commerce and trade very early in history. In the Middle Ages or Renaissance period in Europe, the relationships with its neighbours have always been friendly in the context of trade along the Silk Road. And yet they were a source of exchange between peoples with very different cultures and religions (Buddhists or traditional Chinese religions, Muslims, Christians…), without giving birth to major conflicts or fights for territorial domination. Of course, there were wars in the history of China, but, at the time of its peak, its status of advanced country didn't incite it to conquer territories to make up a global empire. The size of the country was enough. Still, China would have been able to do it: Chinese navigators sailed as far as Africa during the Ming dynasty in the 15th century and Zheng-He explored all south-east Asia and India as far as the Persian Gulf and Somalia. So, despite some expansionist impulses of an emperor or another and military technical capacities with a numerous population allowing to do it, China wisely remained within its borders, its territory being large enough to cover all its needs. The Chinese didn't feel like doing it. Maybe they lacked the adventurous spirit more widespread among European people. In the light of history, we can think that the "Chinese spirit" hasn't changed up to now and that China won't nourish imperialist ambitions as the government so often reminds us of. Anyhow I observe that it wasn't China which caused recent wars to break out everywhere in the world, but the two leaders of the cold war blocks (USA and USSR, later becoming Russia) and our European nations to a lesser extent, since the end of the second world war.

I think that China today is trying to protect itself. The population is still strongly affected by what the western domination imposed upon them during the Opium Wars, the destructions in Beijing (like the looting of the Summer Palace by Anglo-French troops in October 1860, destroying one of the Wonders of the World), or the enforced granting of concessions to France and the United Kingdom in Shanghai (including later the USA and Japan). The population and their leaders know that independence must be won. To my mind, it's probably for that reason that China had a protectionist policy and forbade some activities and societies within its borders (here I think of the American digital giants, the GAFAM) which enabled to strengthen itself and build powerful national champions. But independence can only be economic, otherwise we are in the same situation as the European Union, up to now deprived of a real political strategy and defence policy, always depending on NATO which doesn't only serve its interests. So China can trouble its neighbours who have to alter their view on it: the country was a harmless giant, a laughing matter, and now it's able to defend itself and claim for this fundamental right every nation possesses. China might be a concern for the USA who could view with a jaundiced eye their loss of significant influence in the Pacific. China is often the victim of double speak from great powers: it is accused of being aggressive because it develops its military capacities, but this could be a good thing for a number of countries who don't wish to take military action at international level. The United Nations also welcome a larger contribution of China to the deployment of peacekeepers especially in Africa. Moreover if we speak again of the couple USA-China, which isn't an obsession but on the contrary a good means to compare the two powers, we realize that the budget of the Chinese army is indeed increasing but remains stable in the country's GDP: hardly 2%, sometimes less, sometimes more, since the end of 1980, according to the Stockholm International Peace Research Institute (SIPRI). With the important increase of the Chinese production of wealth, the military expenses have burst out, from 71 billion dollars in 2005 to 200 billion in 2014, their share in the budget varying little. At the same time, countries concerned with that progression, like the USA, spend between 3 and 6% of their GDP in military equipment (in France the military budget is growing but doesn't exceed 2% of GDP). It's true that the expenses of China have grown considerably to become the second country in the world for its military expenses (with an important difference with Russia, number 3), but, once more, it's necessary to examine the situation thoughtfully: China, the first population in the world, always spends three times less than the USA in this matter. It's also very interesting to consult the list of the biggest-spending countries according to SIPRI. Saudi Arabia ranks fourth with 64 billion dollars expenses in 2016, only 5 billion behind Russia. Who is concerned with it and where are the papers headlines denouncing that state of things when Saudi

Arabia is only the 14th GDP in the world? There's a real difference between the two rankings. France, at the sixth place with India being the sixth economic power too, seems to be well-balanced concerning the defence budget. We can also wonder about the absence of Iran in the top 15, as the country is often referred to as a big threat in the Persian Gulf.

If, after all, all that noise about China's military expenses was just a means to weaken the position and credibility of countries which are not the direct allies of traditional dominating powers, i.e. the winners of the Cold War composed of the States, NATO and their allies? Can we be glad about the growing military capacities of the United States, France, India and vilify a similar strategy from China or Russia? The problem might not be those military expenses but political dissensions. China should be pushed aside, considering the potential threat it represents because of its political regime, less reliable than a democracy, however abrupt it might be in its choices. But, in that case, why do we transfer technologies to China and why don't we denounce the military expenses of other regimes, like Saudi Arabia that is second to no one concerning the most coercive regimes? It looks as if, on this point, there is a double standard again. I think the attitude of the west and attempts at coercion on China and Russia are dangerous, as they are felt like aggressions, humiliations and interference. China has its full place in the international community like other countries. It has become a great power again, more active on the international scene, and it shouldn't be rejected on the pretext that its regime is a "threat", which hasn't been confirmed yet.

On the economic front, the feeling of "conquest of the world" or "domination" we sometimes have, is only the consequence of China's place regained in the world economy. The fact that a country with 20% of the world population in the 20th century was so downgraded, was an anomaly. Today the economic catch-up is obvious and might be considered as a threat for a number of countries whose leaders are still living in the old world. In reality, this is not an abnormal situation. China has huge needs but is still far from the end of the road: with about 19% of the world population, its economy still represents only 15% of the global GDP even if this proportion increases each year. China's impact on commodity markets is also important because it needs to feed its industry and therefore the demand of importing countries relying on cheaper Chinese exports. At first glance this domination might seem to be a sign of economic warfare or resource grabbing: China accounts for 59% of world cement production (according to Statista in 2017), 47% of aluminium, 56% of nickel, 50% of steel and copper, 27% of gold or 14% of oil; yet these are only the normal, albeit colossal, needs of the country to keep the economic machine running; the purchase of foreign companies by Chinese groups and the fact they seek to appropriate Western technologies are only one more symptom of a regained financial capacity. This is a fair deal: when a western company that is not a member of the European Union buys or invests in a French company, it's called an investment or a partnership. When it comes to a Chinese society, it's called a wealth grab or a dangerous takeover and one is immediately tempted to think that the Chinese have a more or less sneaky idea behind their heads. Here again there is a lot of prejudice and imagination in my opinion.

All this being said, we mustn't be naïve either: China only defends its national interests, like any self-respecting nation. It will mechanically have more and more weight in the world, economically and militarily. Voluntarily or by force of circumstance, the country will be increasingly involved on the international scene. Some actions will be considered aggressive, such as the development of islands into military complexes in the China Sea, but many other countries, including Western countries, carry out military movements or implement a strategy that is not most friendly, without encountering such fervent shields.

What remains extremely disturbing, at least in my opinion, is the "double standard" treatment. For instance, a few voices are being raised in our country to defend minorities presented as a danger in China, under the right of peoples to self-determination. The Chinese are also always supposed to be submitted to a political regime imposed on them. It's an opinion like any other, but, in that case, what should we think about the reaction of the European Union to the Catalan crisis in 2018? In spite of the fact it seems to be a consequence of the Catalan people's will, the European commission, like the USA and the main European countries reject any idea of separatism in Spain. So there is clearly a difference in treatment on subjects that are ultimately quite comparable: many countries oppose China by all means and would see a forced reunification of Taiwan with mainland China as an affront or even a war declaration, but support Spain and a certain form of repression in defiance of what a majority of Catalans seem to imply.

The Chinese leaders are not stupid and probably not fooled by those strategies either. There is little chance of observing aggressive movements from China because it's in no one's interest. On the contrary, there's room enough to share this world but this will require that our West, and in the first place the USA, accept to renounce certain guarded hunts that the new world order no longer makes legitimate. The administration of the world doesn't belong to a single country and a small court, it's the mission of the United Nations and of a transnational dialogue. I am convinced that the current world will lead us to a sharing of these powers and a certain balance. Let us avoid a too hard alliance game, because it is at this game, that the most devastating conflicts have ended, rarely caused by a single country but rather by a combination of elements, one of the most important of which has always been the renunciation of dialogue and the demonization of a few. It's important to remain firm and not give the keys to a whole region to a single power at the expense of less well-endowed countries, and the role of arbitrator should always remain neutral.

Today and particularly since the election of Donald Trump, there is a strategic space left vacant by the American policy, sometimes described as isolationist, sometimes as a "madman's strategy", with in particular the new modes of expression in invective of President Trump via interposed tweets. As a matter of fact, it's important to note that China's relationships with the United States, two strategic opponents, are not good despite appearances, even if new measures of economic warfare are ignored: the two countries are in opposition on a wide range of issues and they don't trust each other as is shown by the recent classification of China, in December 2017, in the category "hostile opponent of the United States" like Russia, by the way. Though both China and the USA remain pragmatic, the context is unable to warm relations between the two powers, especially concerning trade, as the United States opposed the adoption of

China's status as a market economy in WTO, not to be obliged to reduce customs barriers automatically for Chinese products (barriers that Trump's policy is trying to strengthen today to improve the States' balance of trade, which is quite understandable, but led to tensions on the stock exchange, and , in the end, might not serve the American interests because the price of imported goods will rise). However there's something that our leaders have not yet integrated, it's the peoples' memory, as can easily be seen on social networks, especially in Africa or in Asia: the West, with its colonial and wartime past, is morally disqualified whereas China can conjure up its past and take advantage of its history (particularly in front of crowds of people having an approximate knowledge of Asian history). Rightly or wrongly, it's a fact: the West is subjected to a real guilt and self-flagellation, absent in the Chinese world.

The space left vacant in the leadership of the world shouldn't be seen as a threat. Indeed, it's an opportunity for China, but also for France. It can enable two nations to agree on the essential: defending multilateralism. Assuming that China isn't a bellicose nation (despite some diplomatic clashes, up to now it's not responsible for conflicts outside its borders, and very rarely in history in front of the expansionism of Western countries which is clearly established), it's obvious that France and China, since the presidency of General de Gaulle, have always defended a kind of "third way ", with very different political systems agreeing on promoting multilateralism. At the end of the Second World War, when the future blocks of the Cold War were fixed, that third way represented the countries that didn't wish to side behind the American block or to be dominated by the Soviet bloc. China quickly broke with USSR and understood it had to follow its own way, with difficulties, mistakes and much suffering, as it is generally the case after a revolution when a people undergoes the ups and downs of History. Charles de Gaulle had seen it and he made History in his own way when he was the first among the Western powers to recognize Mao and CCP's China replacing the old nationalist regime that had taken refuge in Taiwan. So, today, that common History, too easily forgotten by our peoples and leaders, can be brought to life again, facilitated by a lesser American commitment in the Pacific. The reinforcement of the European Union is also an important factor for the future France-China relations: a stronger Union will be a synonym for a more independent Union in front of the American policy, and, consequently, more freedom in its strategic choices. The recent declarations of Emmanuel Macron in favour of a European army are in this direction.

To conclude, a third factor is favourable to this rapprochement: as at the peak of China, in the Renaissance period and at the time of Marco Polo's discoveries, the Silk Road can link again the destinies of the Far-East and the West through all the Eurasian continent, via the project of the "new Silk Road", desired and presented by Xi Jinping as soon as 2013. This project, still seen as a project competing with the Western domination, could be a means to reconcile our mutual interests.

10. "NOT LOSING FACE IS THE CHINESE OBSESSION"

People often talk of Chinese being obsessed by "the face", i.e. the fact they have to save face under all circumstances. It belongs to the collective imaginary, like an image repeated regularly but whose meaning very few people understand. It's for me an opportunity to come back to some cultural characteristics in this short chapter dealing with our tenth preconceived idea.

In fact, the "face" is a cultural concept much more subtle than people might think, and important in the relationships between Chinese (not all of them naturally, as it's less observed nowadays among young generations abroad, because of the influence of Western culture) and in business contacts. The "face" notion is generally linked with notions of politeness and respect but pushed to a higher level than being simply polite for Westerners.

Firstly, what is the "face" or the famous "Mian Zi" that is talked of? To simplify, we can say it's the social identity of Chinese people, how someone is perceived in society. The "Mian Zi" includes both the respect due to someone and their "social value". Making someone lose face is embarrassing them in front of others and their own social perception. Making a Chinese lose face results in a loss of his authority, a decrease in his social status and a discomfort that can be long-lasting. Negative effects will follow for the person responsible for it, as far as a pure and simple breakdown of the relationship. Formerly, in the Chinese culture, population movements were rare and

Chinese people would often spend their lives in the same social environment, with the same people around them (friends, family, professional relationships, neighbours). The influence of the Chinese ancestors' culture and local philosophies (like Confucianism, Taoism or Buddhism) resulted in a very important sense of honour and respect which also clearly concerns the respect for authority, elders and teachers. That culture still marks young Chinese, even the least educated living in the most remote provinces.

Nowadays that culture is still very present, and we can easily realize it when we become aware of the important intertwining between work relationships, family and friendships. Any deterioration in an individual's perception can have important consequences in his life, even if, for Westerners, it might seem to be a detail of no importance. A minor detail, a remark, a thoughtless action can take on serious proportions: we must know it, in order to avoid serious misunderstandings.

A word said in a scornful tone, an accusation, an abrupt truth that disturbs, there are so many ways (that do not correspond to the culture of the country) to embarrass people, which will lead to a cold reception, a deterioration of relations or even a break-up. Business contracts have often been lost by foreigners because of their behaviour considered as inappropriate by the Chinese part.

Making him "lose face" or affecting the "Mian Zi" of a Chinese is often the result of some tactless action by someone unaware of it, because they are ignorant of a crucial point in the Chinese culture.

The caricature of this peculiar subject of the Chinese culture, the fact that Chinese people are obsessed by "the face", is quite easy to make but is also quite inaccurate. It's an important aspect of their culture but it doesn't cover all the social relationships in China.

To avoid conflicts all we need to do is showing a minimum of diplomacy, not answering "no" abruptly, and to keep good relationships, giving marks of respect when necessary. Nevertheless, to avoid blunders here are a few practical pieces of advice:

1/ when a contract is going to be signed, it's important to keep the illusion of a shared victory, even if the negotiations have favoured one of the parts. If both parts feel like winning the battle, with a lot of thanks and gestures if necessary, everyone's "Mian Zi" will be respected which is a good thing for all.

2/ concerning relationships with a line manager or someone of a higher social rank, it's important to show signs of respect, like greeting and addressing them first before the other guests. It's a tradition which the other people know, so no need to worry.

3/ during business lunches that are a Chinese tradition regularly respected, the placement at table is important: the person considered as the most important for the event (generally belonging to the highest social rank or having the most power in this business) must be placed in front of the door (when the meal takes place in the private room of a restaurant). The other important people sit next to him. You must be careful not to offend anyone when placing them. During the meal the best dishes must be passed to this person first, and to drink a toast (which takes place many times during the meal, not only at the beginning as in the West) you can get up and go to him and then do the toast with your glass slightly under his, as a sign of respect. This is greatly appreciated, all the more as you are placed far from him. You can also simply tap the table with the foot of your glass after nodding to the person you wish to pay your respects to.

4/ in the Chinese culture, it's customary not to defy authority: don't ask a teacher too many questions not to make him feel ill-at-ease or lose face if he can't answer a question that would be too precise or difficult. Moreover, direct criticism is to be banished, all the more so if it happens in front of witnesses, which, in such a case, would be a serious offence.

5/ relationship with time is important: taking one's time is not a mark of indecision in China, on the contrary. It shows reflection and time is necessary to make wise decisions as was customary in the ancestral culture. It's a positive attitude appreciated in China, implicitly showing that one doesn't want to disturb the natural order of things and isn't part of a logic of rupture. In business dealings, it's also better not to be in a hurry, which might be a sign of greed and considered as a desire to take advantage of partners.

6/ it's also better not to press one's partner, not to be as direct as in the West. To be arrogant or critical must be banished too. Punctuality in relationships is also important. Even if it's possible to be late in some particular cases, being late without apologizing is really impolite.

7/ too abrupt judgements on China, concerning some local cultural aspects or someone, are very impolite too.

8/ lastly, humour can be used, but carefully, it mustn't be too acid or ironical as it is sometimes in Europe, in some case it would not be understood or could cause misunderstanding. Laughing at the expense of a partner must be avoided, but a congenial humour that values him is appreciated. American people are generally better than Europeans at this game because their cultural habits reject forms of stigmatizing humour.

In the context of our personal or business travels in China, we are not prepared to know those cultural differences, which is quite common and gives birth to mistakes and, sometimes, serious misunderstandings. However, with the best will and trying to be as polite as possible, a faux pas can easily be made in a situation that our partner doesn't understand or misinterprets. Our Judeo-Christian culture, which is materialistic and individualist with a high level of critical thinking, is very different from the Chinese culture, and even when we are aware of the differences and the mistakes we must avoid, we may always make some, unconsciously, as it is a cultural reflex.

Nevertheless, we mustn't focus on the attitudes to banish, or criticize all those rules that might seem secondary. In fact, in behaving well with a lot of observation, it's quite possible to adapt oneself to Chinese partners in a benevolent way to avoid confusions and embarrassing situations for both sides. Because of those many subtleties in relationships, it is in fact quite easy for a foreign observer to make a mockery of those cultural habits and manners, which brings us to the next preconceived idea in relation with the last aspects mentioned.

11. "CHINESE PEOPLE ARE OBSEQUIOUS"

After the chapter on « Mian Zi », the time has come to tackle another preconceived idea: « the Chinese are obsequious ». We all keep in mind caricatures, dating back more or less from the 19th or the beginning of the 20th centuries, showing a grinning Chinese with long nails, a plait, smiling frantically and walking backwards bowing like a servant, describing all his services as "miserable", not to mention his hands joined in broad sleeves. So, it looks like a Chinese at the end of the Qing era, the last Manchu dynasty (1644-1912), or a Chinese from the "Tintin and Snowy" cartoons albums, though the caricature wasn't as strong as in the description we have just made which does no credit to it.

In spite of China's modernization and the evolution of its ways of life, it's an image that people often have in mind: the image of the obsequious, double-dealing Chinese or a mixture of the two, too polite to be honest and who never says what he thinks. It's a worrying picture which, despite a few underlying features mentioned before when we spoke of "Mian Zi", is far from reality. We are going to try and understand by what cultural and character features the Chinese have been catalogued, and in a more pleasant way, we will profit by the opportunity to give some advice (concerning the right attitude to have) to people wishing to travel in China and build relationships there. We have already discussed how the Chinese toast, which is different from our Western habits, even if the principle remains the same. We can come back to some aspects and deal with the fact of toasting in a more precise cultural way. As I said before, respect is a central value in China and a very important component of social relations. Drinking spirits isn't as common in China as in France or the rest of Europe (except for light alcoholic drinks like beer for instance): a Chinese rarely drinks a glass of wine alone, as a Frenchman can do, wine being for him an element of culture and 'terroir' as important as the content of his plate. In China, wines and spirits are generally reserved for great occasions like family meals or, more frequently, business lunches. For more simple meals among friends, apart from tea, beer is more popular. In the West the guests toast at the beginning of the meal and greet each other with "cheers", whereas the Chinese toast through the entire meal. It's true that there is a moment at the beginning of the meal when they toast collectively as in France. But afterwards, the meal often goes on in the same way. The most important guest is rarely the first to toast someone else, except in particular cases, to highlight their presence, value them or thank them. In a business meal, the one we can call the claimant (those who is seeking to build the relation) will be the first to toast the most important one. Three possibilities exist, depending on the level of respect one wants to show towards their guest. The first attitude is the most respectful: the claimant gets up and walks towards the important guest. Before doing so, he'd better have checked the glasses are full of wine (red wine generally, called by the Chinese "hong putao jiu" meaning red grapes wine; another alcoholic drink would certainly be "Moutai" (pronounced 'Mou tai jiu'), an expensive sorghum alcohol much sought after, reaching 45° and which is served in small glasses they drink in one go). When he is in front of his "target", the claimant bows slightly and pronounces the fetish sentence: "Gan Bei!" (Literally it means "dry glass", an equivalent for our "cheers!" everywhere or "Santé!" in France). Moving oneself really shows the degree of respect towards a guest. When you toast, you must take care that your glass is a little under your guest's, once more to show your respect: you are "under" him in this situation. You can add a few compliments and wishes to the action before drinking, and express thanks, then go back to your place or do the same action with another guest in order of "importance".

The second technique is quite similar and can be adopted if the recipient isn't too far on the seating plan. Remaining seated, you turn to him (crossing his eyes and nodding your head while raising your glass will be clear enough) and toast him with your glass under his own.

Lastly, the third technique can be used if you don't wish to show too much deference, or at the end of the meal after several toasts. In China, meals often take place at the restaurant in private rooms where the food is placed on a glass turntable (due to the number of shared dishes, which is very different from the western style). So, in such a situation, you can toast without getting up, looking at the recipient and saying "gan bei" tapping the bottom of the glass on the table two or three times before raising it to your lips. This is toasting from a distance, like a kiss sent by the hand in our countries.

On the same subject, table placing is particularly important. We have already mentioned it before but it can be useful to speak of it again: it may seem unimportant but still is crucial in China as a source of misunderstanding and a bad signal. The most important guest must be placed in front of the entrance door of the private room where the meal takes place at the restaurant (it's highly improbable that a business lunch should be organized in the collective room, too noisy and lacking discretion. The other important guests for the success of the meal are placed on his right and on his left. The person who invites can sit in front of him, with his back to the door; a place which isn't much appreciated but very useful to give instructions for the service. As a sign of respect, there's no need to make long speeches; some cultural knowledge on the attitude to adopt for a Westerner will be highly appreciated: for example, showing his place clearly without sitting down before him, being considerate to him by passing on the best dishes. All this, for a layman's eye, can be considered as obsequious, but it's only a cultural attitude which mustn't be misunderstood. Valuing someone doesn't imply a personal devaluation but, on the contrary, is a simple means to show that the relationship is of particular concern to us. By the way, it's crucial to have the same attitude with the people accompanying the important guest, especially if they are members of his family (except, of course, the fact of toasting and drinking spirits with children, which would be senseless). In China it's quite common to see family and business relations inextricably linked. Your guest may introduce you with his wife or one of his children and you'll have to show them the same consideration. Lastly, when it comes to paying there's no question of sharing. The bill must be given to you exclusively and, then, you'll pay discreetly to a server. If someone suggests to share the bill, you must refuse, several times if necessary, smiling and saying "mei shi". The Chinese can insist, but it doesn't mean they really want to pay, it's just a form of politeness. Equally, when you invite someone to do something like filling a glass or sharing a dish, they can say "no".

Quite often, it can be a polite "no" and doesn't mean they really wish to refuse. You can insist, kindly smiling, or you can serve them directly. A real refusal may be visible then, or they can simply not finish their glass. It is not a very complicated custom either.

Wishes are another social aspect in China. By "wishes" I mean the phrases used to toast or to wish a good year, a good birthday or success in business. It's necessary for people going to China and having professional contacts or business lunches, to know some of them. Even if you don't speak Chinese well, one or two wishes, at the right moments, will highlight your attention to detail, respect and sympathy for your partner as well as for the traditions and customs of China and its inhabitants. Many foreigners are content to be polite and attentive (which is already quite appreciable, compared with some inappropriate attitudes of tourists and businesspeople on the edge of rudeness and behaving like in conquered territory). These phrases, attitudes and very basic knowledge of Chinese manners will make the difference appreciably. Let's now review some wishes.

The Chinese have a list of several dozen common wishes, and positive things people wish one another. They can be expressed in a more or less literary way, and are, in fact, polite formulas. Generally, they are ready-made sentences which could be compared to our traditional "happy new year, wishing you good health" with a little more subtlety perhaps. A personal touch can always be added to them. It's a social convention, a sign of courtesy, and the ideal is to answer back, thanking and wishing some good thing in turn.

On the occasion of the Chinese New Year, first, the basic "Xin nian hao" meaning "new year good" or "xin nian kuai le" meaning "new year happy". They can be used indifferently for January 1st, the new year of the Gregorian calendar. For these wishes, the expressions "Zhu ni" or "Zhu nin" (when you want to show more respect, as if you were addressing a boss or a teacher in China) mean "I wish you". A whole sentence expressing a wish could be "Zhu ni xin nian kuai le": I wish you a happy new year!

According to the Chinese sign of the year, you can be more elaborate. For instance, as the year 2018 was the year of the dog, you could wish "Gou nian da ji": "lucky dog year". "Gou" (dog) can very well be replaced by one of the other eleven signs of Chinese astrology and used for every New Year. You must be careful not to use the wrong sign because Chinese people are often superstitious. The signs of the Chinese Zodiac are, by order, the rat (lao shu), the ox (niu), the tiger (lao hu), the rabbit (tu zi), the dragon (long), the snake (shi), the horse (ma), the goat (yang), the monkey (hou zi), the rooster (ji), the dog (gou), and the pig (zhu). Another way to wish the New Year might be "Gong he xin xi" (an equivalent for happy new year) or the popular "Wan shi ru yi" (happiness for this year). Several wishes can be expressed together, preceded by "Zhu ni" (or "Zhu nimen", if the wishes are addressed to several people).

Other wishes concerning health, work, financial success, can be added. On a birthday, you can say "Shenti jian kang" meaning "good health" (literally "body health"). Or "Sheng ri kuai le" (happy birthday "birth day happy").

For business success wishes, "Gong xi fa cai" should be preferred, meaning something like "wish for wealth", or "wish for prosperity". It is also often used in the New Year as a wish for people invested in business and hoping success, whereas the "shenti jian kang" is rather a wish for the elderly. Maybe a last cultural anecdote, concerning the New Year wishes, can be useful too: a more literary wish is "Fu lu shou", a wish for happiness and prosperity in the Chinese tradition. "Fu Xing" is in China the god of luck often pictured as a learned old man dressed in traditional clothes (a mandarin costume) and holding a parchment. "Shou Xing" is the god of longevity. "Lu" refers to the pay of a Mandarin and also represents notoriety as well as respect due to a high position. "Fu Lu Shou" is the summary of these symbols enabling to wish longevity and prosperity. This is an illustration of all the richness of the Chinese language which makes it possible to reveal very complex ideas and references in a very short way, that you can only understand if you have received a formal education. This wish mustn't be preceded by "Zhu ni".

Finally, to get it over with wishes (this book isn't a complete Chinese referential), it may be useful to mention travel wishes. When you leave your family or friends for a long travel, you can wish them "Yi lu ping an" or "Yi lu shun feng" meaning "Have a good trip". The first expression literally means "peace on the way", and the second one rather means "god trip with favourable winds", which isn't to be used for travels by plane. As mentioned before, the Chinese are rather superstitious and winds and planes are not compatible in the same sentence, especially for a wish.

Thanking is also important in China but not in the same way as in the West. Once more it is a peculiar aspect which was misinterpreted and later made us think that Chinese people are obsequious. The reality is quite different. In China everyone can notice that they thank their hosts very much but less their relatives. They thank their business relations very much but less their friends. In fact, thanking is used with strangers, not just anyone but people they have a minimum of relationships with. In the streets, with people holding the door, thanking isn't very common, due to the large population in Chinese cities and some individualism that slowly destroys social relations (considering the urban conditions of life, as can be seen in Paris too, on a smaller scale). With their families or friends, the Chinese speciality is to help one another. I think that saying "thank you" isn't really necessary because helping or serving someone physically is considered as natural. For very close relations, it can even be considered as strange to thank too much. Personally, I have seen members of the family, sometimes not so close, travelling hundreds of kilometres to bring their help or take us somewhere by car and refusing to hear any thanks. Helping is also a means to show one's attachment without expecting anything in return. This is selflessness without any obsequiousness. On the other hand, thanking is indispensable in the intermediate stages of relationships like business contacts. Showing carefully one's appreciation for each small gesture is a necessity, particularly when trying to do business with someone who less needs your services than you do. This is basic politeness, even if it may seem exaggerated to us in the West.

A last aspect is generosity. We have already spoken of money, but Chinese politeness also consists in bringing presents when they meet or see someone again (except for close friends with whom a certain proximity or relaxation has settled in), even if it may seem there is no particular reason to make a present. It is true for the family but also for other more distant relationships. And, generally, the gifts are beautiful. For a wedding, the people close to the bride and groom from each family (uncles, aunts, brothers and sisters, and their parents of course) often exchange gifts, so it is very embarrassing to arrive empty-handed. You have certainly noticed that Chinese people, when they travel, spend a lot. In fact, most of their purchases are not for their personal use, as we mentioned it earlier in another chapter. There are orders placed by relatives or neighbours who don't have the opportunity of travelling, but most of the purchases are generally made for their families or their friends. Once more, it's not money that is important but how it is used. In France people will bring you a magnet as a souvenir and it will be nice to have had a thought for the person who will receive it. In China, if they can afford it, it will be Hermès scarves (French luxury being relatively less expensive in France than in China) for everybody, knowing that those who receive will later also make beautiful gifts. Everything in its time and relationships and "Mian Zi" will be well kept.

We have seen that there are a lot of different ways to be polite, to wish good things and respect uses in China. All this is only a brief overview. These different uses and social conventions are very common in China and don't take much time to be executed, but they might suggest some obsequiousness for an uninformed eye. It's simply a matter of showing a minimum of respect to the person you are talking to (if he or she deserves it of course) or honouring his or her host. All these uses are often a way of providing a service or seeking social support: when you are looking for a service from a powerful person or if you want to do business, you sometimes have to be a little flattering. This is part of the game and all parties know it well.

Therefore, there is no obsequiousness in these behaviours and social uses, and no more background thoughts than in the West either. Social pressure and politeness in China are even much less important in China than in other countries or for other cultures, in Asia or elsewhere, in Japan in particular. I hope it has been demonstrated in this chapter.

12. "CHINA IS HYPOCRITICAL AND PLUNDERS THE WEST ECONOMICALLY"

In reality there are two statements in the title of this new chapter. The first one, often heard, underlines the so-called "double standards" of China with third countries (generally we speak here of Europe and France in particular). The second statement is a little more complex, as it implies that China uses the weapons of the West against that same geographic and cultural entity. Let's take stock of the facts and what may actually raise questions.

Concerning the "economic plundering", we often refer to the purchase of land (in France several cases were reported between 2015 and 2018), agricultural land most of the time. Chinese investments in Europe are often mentioned too: in large companies, in infrastructures (Port of Piraeus in Athens, Greece; holdings in airport companies as in Toulouse, France) or in traditional jewels such as the Bordeaux wine estates. All this is true of course: Chinese nationals connected to Chinese people or companies owned by Chinese people, make business in foreign countries and, according to the rules of our open economies, can buy land or local companies. Every country has its own laws, but we chose, years ago, to be open countries, respecting private property and governed by market and free trade rules (with safeguards, it's not the Far West and, in spite of many approximations, we cannot do as we like: rules exist, though often forgotten by commentators). These laws are sometimes misused with discreet purchases of agricultural land, that do not directly concern the land itself, through shares of companies that own the land. The risk of a transfer of national land assets is real, but in such a case, it's always possible to declare the purchase of land by foreign capital illegal, without distinction, on the grounds of national interest. A law would be enough, but it would be better to know how to use the existing tools that are supposed to protect the land, like the Safer mechanism in France (societies that oversee rural and land development and can have a pre-emptive right to defend French agriculture and land), but, in an incomprehensible way, they are incompetent when the sale isn't about the land itself but about a company owning the land as long as the shares purchased don't represent 100% of the total shares. In other words, as a foreigner, I can buy 99% of an agricultural area by purchasing the company owning and operating it, and no limits can be set against me. So we can criticize Chinese people and other foreign investors, but there are sellers who benefit from it too, and I think we hold out the stick to get beaten through ineffective protection systems. A consultation is planned, it seems, in the senate in the coming months to try and find a legal solution to this land problem. This notion of "economic plundering" is, now and then, mentioned for French companies setting up in China: joint ventures are necessary and it's a good means for Chinese companies to have access to the know-how and technologies of western groups. It's partly for this reason that Chinese companies developed so quickly: first inspiration with possible copying, then innovation. First, they do it less well and cheaper, then as well and always cheaper, and finally better and cheaper or at the same price. So, a feeling of injustice may prevail, which is legitimate on the part of some European or American people, but the groups desiring to set up in China directly know the rules already when they accept them to enter that market. And they accept them despite the inconveniences because they want to have a chance to take advantage of the enormous potential of the Chinese market with important short and middle-term profits (and production conditions at a lower cost than in the West, which, by the way, is detrimental to our jobs and industry). We can't win on all fronts, or in that case we just simply export, which cannot be applied to all productions.

I think we mustn't be naïve in commercial transactions. In March 2018, an article from the "Research Foundation Flanders" pointed out very appropriately the rather foolish situation of Europe in relation to China in terms of trade deficit and technology transfer. The author called for a strong European reaction, even aggressive, noting that European economic and political elites had been mistaken about China for more than twenty years. To begin with, a first cultural and political mistake: the West expected more democracy and that China would naturally move towards those famous "universal values" so dear to our European and North-American allies. It was a serious mistake, as we can see today that the country isn't following that way and isn't the only one. The second mistake that the author perfectly noticed was the great naivety of economic decision-makers to suppose they could delocalize low-cost production while specializing in technology and value-added products. In 2018, when we look at the level of technical progress of Chinese products, we realize that China doesn't only copy bur innovates in almost every field: energy, digital, telecommunications, artificial intelligence, transport…All sectors are on the way to being controlled. If this is the case, there is a lack of solutions. It's easy to criticize and declare that "the Chinese are stealing from us" but it shows nothing more than the frustration of the Old World unable to go on dominating the emerging new powers in the making. This is not completely wrong, but our own naivety to focus on short-term profit has made us fail on that field. But are we playing in the same time scale? Our democracies think of five- or ten-year periods of time according to the rhythm of mandates and political support. China projects itself fifty years into the future, owing to its political system, perfectly stable, at least until today. Once again, time flows differently in old China.

However, does it mean that China is engaged in economic plundering? What do western countries exactly think? Should a business partner give us free gifts when they had and still have a development gap to fill? "Sweet trade" is obviously a utopia, but it's all the more obvious as negative impacts affect us. Clearly China does its best to take advantage of its business relationships with Europe and the United States (which try to react at least, maybe not always choosing the best way, like Trump threatening to increase custom duties on some products, a threat to which China is responding, but with a delay as usual). It's as if our countries had forgotten the lessons of the past, when we were on the best side of the fence. Not such a long time ago, hardly 150 years back, France and England had forced China to open up at the end of the nineteenth century, in order to be able to engage in the lucrative trafficking of opium, and make some profit without regard for the consequences on the country and its population. Forced drug dealing in some way.

Instead of establishing facts, sometimes in a simplistic way, sometimes more finely according to the media expressing them, it would be interesting to think about solutions like, for instance, the third way to follow. It might be some limited protectionism, protecting parts of our economies from China, and also from all our business partners outside the European Union. The United States seem to have already understood. This, coupled with diplomacy in the service of Europe and not modelled on North-American diplomacy, could be beneficial, as our interests, in the old continent, are not identical to those of the USA in particular. This also raises the question of the role of NATO today and the lack of a common defence policy in Europe. We would benefit from a refocusing of Europe which could clearly profit by closer ties with both China and Russia, a link between Europe and Asia. Why should it mean, as we are often opposed to, abandoning the close ties that bind us to the peoples of European culture in North America, our long-standing allies?

As a conclusion, I don't think China is more hypocritical than any other country. China plays its part, and I think it is normal for our economies, which are not well prepared for the new emergence of such giants, to feel concerned. We have taken advantage of cheap products for years and we are still taking advantage of them, but we have sacrificed long-term strategy and many local jobs on the altar of competitiveness. Nowadays the consumers pay attention to the price first because they often have no other choice. Some people would like to promote employment in France and Europe as well as better environmental standards while reducing the impact of transport of goods, but the power of the low price is such that any change seems impossible. We'll see, in the event of a protectionist policy, the effect on the purchase power of consumers, but for some industries it's already too late because there is no longer any production capacity left in our countries. Under these conditions and for these productions, a recovery in the trade balance seems to be a real challenge and the subject is too complex to be dealt here with in a few lines. China, like others, is profiting by its strategic advantages and the free scope given to it within the framework of the WTO of which it is a full member since 2001. Global economic competition is fierce, and everyone is looking to benefit from it, some countries doing it better than others because they are better equipped or more pragmatic and more strategic in the long run, helped by their huge internal markets. Can we accuse them of hypocrisy when this game is played by everyone?

What to think of the CIA, FBI and NSA's statements at the beginning of 2018 asking the Americans not to use Huawei's products and seeking to obtain the outright ban of the brand in government or civil servant equipment because of doubts about possible espionage or collection of sensitive data, whereas American companies like Apple or Microsoft are not attacked in the same way when they also hold millions of sensitive data on their European or Asian customers, some of which are directly communicated to the NSA and therefore to a foreign government? What about the wiretap cases set up by a previous administration that collected data from the personal phones of German Chancellor Angela Merkel? After a little noise, nothing happened and there were no formal attacks on a possible hypocrisy of our allies. Once again, China probably acts in the same way because that's how our fully competitive world works, and it shouldn't shock anyone: it's a legitimate strategy put in place by the various sovereign countries, but China is often more easily attacked in a diplomacy dominated by double standards. It's this state of things that I choose to denounce, hoping less naivety from our commentators in the future. A complex world requires at least as complex an analysis, which doesn't simply break down open doors for the pleasure of it.

13. "THE HAN MAJORITY ETHNIC GROUP CRUSHES THE OTHERS. BESIDES, THE CHINESE ARE RACIST"

We often hear very harsh analyses on the Chinese population and in particular on the Hans who, as mentioned in a previous chapter, are the majority ethnic group. It is estimated that they represent 92% of the Chinese population, i.e. about 1.2 billion people. It should be noted that this ethnic group, whose origins date back at least to the first millennium BC, is also widespread on the island of Taiwan, as well as in Indonesia and in Singapore. In the world there are many representatives of the Han ethnic group: this is at least 1.3 billion individuals, almost one in five people on our planet. It's undoubtedly the largest, if not homogeneous, ethnic group of humans on earth. Of course, among them are cultures that can vary as well as different physical characteristics (between a northern Chinese, a Cantonese and an eastern Chinese we will have differences that are sometimes notable), nevertheless the Hans do indeed form a majority ethnic group not only in mainland China but also in Taiwan, Hong-Kong, Singapore and in parts of Malaysia.

Now this majority ethnic group in China is often accused (little in China of course but especially in the West) of crushing the other ethnic groups present in East Asia and in China in particular. Apart from the fact that this should only lead to cautious comments from Westerners, if there is to be a comment, it's also fundamentally false. Of course, the Hans are over-represented because they account for more than 90% of the population in mainland China. Moreover, this proportion has tended to gradually decrease. Wouldn't it be strange for a group presented as overwhelming and dominating? I'll try here to present some examples showing that the Hans's reputation for excessive domination, in addition to its natural weight, remains well exaggerated and, in my opinion, largely undeserved.

The first observation to be made is the gradual decrease in the proportion of Hans in the Chinese population. Why, are you going to tell me? It's the consequence of the one-child policy decided under Deng Xiaoping in 1979 during the country's major modernizations which caused a real accelerated demographic transition at the end of the twentieth century in China. But, when they accuse the Hans, many people neglect the fact that this policy was aimed precisely at the Hans, to protect the Chinese ethnic minorities and other cultures. In the country, ethnic minorities have a real status and are somehow sacralised. The constitution of the People's Republic of China officially recognizes 56 of them.

So, the important ethnic minorities like Turkish-speaking Uighurs and north-west Muslims in Xinjiang, Manchus in the north-east (an area covered by 3 provinces: Jilin, Heilongjiang and Liaoning), Tibetans in Tibet autonomous province, Miaos in the south (province of Yunnan), have kept the possibility of having more children than the Hans, as provided for by the birth control policy that has been vigorously maintained in mainland China for nearly 40 years. Ethnic minorities were therefore not concerned, which is already a first sign of the respect shown to them by the Central State but also, and this is the main one, of the concern for the rebalancing of certain forces by the authorities. The population had to be reduced in order to allocate the meagre resources of the time to economic growth, but this sacrifice had to come from the dominant population in the figures: the Hans. Today we have probably reached the low point of the Han proportion in the total population of China. As a matter of fact, the one-child policy has been greatly relaxed or even lifted and now the Hans are at almost the same level as the other ethnic minorities. Some cultural differences may still exist, as among the Uighurs, who traditionally have more children, but they won't reduce the proportion of Hans that will remain overwhelming anyway. In the big urban areas in the east of China, the Han population is even more dominant and has a very low fertility rate, most parents refusing to have a second or a third child despite the real possibility provided by the government. So, the weight of minorities will probably remain stable for a long time, at about 8% of the total population. These minorities, which have often been defended without understanding the real ins and outs of the situation, a little in the French tradition, strongly inspired by the attitude of David against Goliath (automatically defending the people that are considered as the weakest), benefit from sometimes significant advantages. Indeed, there is a lot of talk about Tibet and Xinjiang because of the settlement of many Hans in this province but it should be noted that these movements are encouraged by the government to develop these provinces in particular. Maybe the central government has another idea in mind, but it's impossible to prove and, in my opinion, rather difficult to imagine, whatever we can say about it. On the other hand, they have always wanted to balance living standards and economic growth between the provinces by reducing differences from one province to another in a centralized way. We have done so in France too, in our regions, by pushing for decentralization throughout the second half of the twentieth century.

There are many reasons for it, and we can just mention the will to stem the rural exodus, the over densification of cities (it is estimated that about 300 million rural workers have migrated to the eastern metropolitan areas, putting immense pressure on them), or the quest for stability in the immense territory filled with contrasts (and constraints) that is China. So the Hans, settling in provinces with a high proportion of ethnic minorities, don't do so to dominate them or whatever reason that will suit the defenders of separatist claims, but because they are economically and fiscally encouraged for the final benefit of the entire province. It's a Chinese way of applying the theory of the invisible hand of the market, where the sum of the special interests of the "homo economicus" leads to the benefit of the general interest.

I have therefore never detected a hint of contempt or an ounce of colonialism in the way the Hans see their compatriots from other ethnic groups or living in more remote provinces without demerit. Of course some people living in Shanghai or Beijing will be the first to complain about the "invasion" of some "peasants" (other Hans in 95% of cases in fact), but this is due to a cultural gap and attitudes that are unacceptable in the most developed parts of China, and not because of remarks coming from some latent racism. In addition to the former pro-family policy, China grants facilities to ethnic minorities, sometimes to the detriment of the Hans. Without even mentioning autonomy in certain parts of the territory that has been granted to one or the other minority, important advantages exist to restore a certain equality of opportunity among the Chinese people. We can even talk of positive discrimination, an example being the entrance exam to the best universities: for equal performance, a student who is a member of recognized ethnic minority will pass a Han or a student from an economically more privileged city or province. This system is a little similar to what exists in the USA and can shock a European, given the racialist nature of the procedure but this is how it works: a black person will need a lower score to enter an Ivy League university than a Hispanic person who will need a lower score than a white person, who himself will need a lower score than an Asian person (comparison of SAT scores based on a complaint lodged by 64 associations in 2015). It seems that President Trump is now seeking to question this principle.

So, to return to China, if the dominant Han ethnic group crushed the others, why would the government have put in place such procedures? Wouldn't it be easier to wait a few decades for the disappearance or outright marginalization of these minorities, which are supposed to be so embarrassing although they weigh so little on the country's population? Wouldn't it be easier to do so without being challenged, in a truly censored and authoritarian state? The truth is that the central government is trying to gradually eliminate differences between the provinces, not for the beauty of this action, but to level up the provinces where life is still difficult. Culturally it will probably be impossible and not necessarily desirable or desired, but the government is thus trying to attract minorities to a way of life that is fully included in the Chinese economic and social life, based until now on the Hans' society. Personally, it's difficult for me to oppose this in the light of our French traditions, ardently defending the integration of all in a single model represented by the values of the Republic centred on assimilation. Everyone knows that the success of such a policy is sometimes relative, but the technique remains the same: to make a people it's necessary to unify it or even standardize it; so, we can imagine the heavy task this represents for a country as diverse as China (France went through this process when its territory was unified and the French language was imposed, which didn't prevent it from leaving alone territories with a strong identity, such as Corsica, for example), which isn't a federation of nations but a unitary state able to grant some autonomy to its minorities but not to cede entire parts of territory for separatist claims. This is done to the great displeasure of idealists who misunderstand the constraints weighing on China, those who one day reveal themselves against Catalonia's independence despite a popular vote, but who come out in favour of the secession of Chinese provinces, a country that never interferes in the internal affairs of its partners.

Now let's come to the second part of our title sentence: are the Chinese people racist? For some, China and the Chinese will always remain the devil, which is, of course, misunderstood by the inhabitants of the country, but one accusation often made is that of racism. It's a question taken very seriously, especially by the Chinese themselves, who sometimes, it's true, note the clumsiness of their compatriots. Is there a real Chinese racism? At the particular level, I'm afraid there's no answer to this question because there will always be harmful beliefs conveyed by ignorance. At the general level, however, the answer is, as everyone can imagine, no.

Several controversies have been in the news in recent years: sometimes an advertisement for washing-powder deemed racist, sometimes a report on African victims of racism in Guangzhou, or even more recently a short sketch during the major Chinese New Year television event, taking place in Africa with a number of clumsiness.

It's easy to describe the Chinese as racist, self-centred, ignoring others. In my opinion this is far from accurate. All those controversies are, it's true, served by still inappropriate behaviour due to the lack of cultural coexistence of the Chinese living in China. Ignorance of the morals of foreigners (and specifically of non-Western foreigners) is rather widespread in the country, which leads to prejudices that are inappropriately expressed and are clumsier than racist. Obviously, a sticky behaviour towards black tourists (which can still be observed outside the big cities) will, of course, be embarrassing: whoever wants to be taken to task, pointed out or continuously disturbed for pictures by strangers? It's rather curiosity that prevails and not animosity. Again, this analysis doesn't prejudge individual behaviour.

As a conclusion, I am convinced that the Chinese citizen is no more racist than any other inhabitant of our world. Unlike us in the West, he lives in a world that is much less politically correct in this respect. Opinions that are sometimes on the verge of racism can be expressed fairly freely, sometimes disapproved of by another interlocutor, whether in a traditional discussion forum or via social networks, which are not lacking in pearls on this subject. In our country, in spite of a society that is much more mixed than Chinese society, there are still many prejudices. They are simply less expressed. I am sure that with a little adaptation time and an ever-greater openness of the country, China will no longer be accused of being populated by racists. It already proves it by the way it treats Africa on its territory: as equals and not as a colonial power, without getting involved politically and without giving lessons of "civilization".

Add-on in December 2019 about the situation in Xinjiang

In Europe and in the US, the year 2019 has been marked by a lot of communication about China and especially 1/ Hong Kong (already discussed earlier), and 2/ Xinjiang and the situation with the Uyghurs.

It has become of public knowledge that large facilities (some media already call them 'concentration camps', without shame…) have been build in the province of Xinjiang for some Uyghurs, the native of the minority ethnic group of this region. Uyghurs are close to Turkish people in their culture and language, and most of them are of Muslim faith.

The true is that we don't know much about these places. The central government has called them 'education camps', western media often use the term 'prison-camps'. Some Chinese representatives call them 'fake news' or exaggerations, other just consider they are part of a re-education program in a context of social unrest and terrorism.

The truth is that Xinjiang and Muslim separatists have indeed been directly involved in terrorist attacks in China. The most well-known attack is the Kunming attack in 2014, were more than 30 people were killed with long-bladed knives by radical Islamic terrorists (Xinjiang's Uyghur people) at the Kunming railway station in the province of Yunnan, China. Around 140 people were also injured in the attack. Other attacks have been perpetrated in China, in 2010 (Aksu bombing), in 2011 (Hotan attack and Kashgar attack), in 2014 in Urumqi. As it is the case in other parts of the world and in the West, China is thus also confronted with radical Islam and terrorism, and the government has identified terrorism as one of the "three-evils" harming the country.

This is in this context that the Central Government has decided to watch more closely what was happening in Xinjiang, as some of the citizens of this autonomous region had also left the country to go to Syria or Iraq when ISIS (the so-called Islamic State that still killed more Muslims than people of any other belief) was still attracting would-be terrorists.

As a result, re-education complexes were built and thousands of Xinjiang people (mostly young people) were sent to a program for several weeks, aimed at avoiding radical religion in order to avoid further crimes. I rely on what was described, and no foreign journalist has been there to check (but still lots of them claim to know the truth).

This re-education program seems to have widened in 2018-2019, with some numbers told by European and American newspapers of about 1 million people in these camps. It could be true, but it seems to be huge (5% of the Xinjiang population), at least not at the same time. And there is no report of crimes committed or loss of lives, so the comparison with Nazi camps seems to be totally out of proportion, to say the least.

What is striking in this affair, is the speed at which the West took conclusions. China was immediately guilty. But we seem to forget that Europe was also struck (and is still struck) by terrorism: in Paris, Berlin, Brussels, Strasbourg, Nice, London…even in the US. What have we done to try to stop it and to protect our citizens? The US has created Guantanamo (not a model of rule of law), and Europe has reacted as well: in France, the 'State of Emergency' law permitted easier arrests, and lots of suspects were directly jailed. China has its own way to deal with these crimes and the government is perfectly aware that Xinjiang could have been the perfect place for a new civil war: Muslims vs. non-Muslims, and China, sometimes viewed as a threat to western countries, would be heavily handicapped for a long time… China will never allow a new Syria on its territory.

Still, as a matter of fact, no terrorist attack has been recorded in China since 2017 and the beginning of this affair. The international community must not tolerate any harsh measure taken by any country, even in its own sovereign territory, but this harassment of China, week after week, seems to me like a preparation of the western opinion for a next step. There are real horrors taking place in our world, but the paper is always more easily sold when it's about China. All means seem good to provoke international anger towards this country.

This week, at the end of the year 2019, CNN has now announced a new breaking news: 'China has been destroying Uyghur cemeteries at an accelerated rate'. Of course, the conclusion was again that Han Chinese are racist. But what can you say to Shanghainese people, or Beijing inhabitants, when their traditional homes were destroyed in order to construct new buildings? Was that racism again? We often forget that new China is still under construction, and lots of traditional places have been altered or destroyed in the process.

Also, it's easy to say that these actions in Xinjiang are against Muslims. But that is forgetting that religions are not free to preach as they want in China. The same is true for Protestants, Catholics, and other faiths. For many people in China, foreign religions are still considered with caution. It is no different than in many other countries and, again, to my view, this is a political choice and right of any government to do so.

14. "CHINA IS AN UNEQUAL COUNTRY"

People often say that China is an unequal country and it is vilified for this reason. There are truly wide disparities between people across the country. But, is the picture so black? Is it right to focus on these inequalities and to constantly rebuff an entire country for it, while making fun or deliberately mocking some of its inhabitants? For a fair return of things, it would be interesting to analyse the situation of China on this point and to return to more objective findings in order not to fall into the fairly common fantasy of the country of all defects, whatever they may be.

Historically (our reader knows it perfectly now), the Middle Kingdom, which became the Republic of China then the People's Republic of China, has never been the land of equality. With thousands of year-old traditions, with marked social separations, China has never known these wills of egalitarianism, now very fashionable and belonging to the famous universal self-proclaimed values and guarantees of the thought of a part of the West. These are certainly imprinted with humanism but they seek to impose themselves through diplomacy and the often clumsy lessons of our democracies, which are always ready to correct the misguided by preaching values that they themselves no longer practice or, in any case, by following their own measures. This observation doesn't apply only to China, because it's true that Western countries often act as lecturers towards former colonies or countries less rich than themselves or culturally different. Why don't the inhabitants and governments of those countries follow the best possible path, that of our famous "universal values"? To depart from this rule would necessarily be negative, without taking into account the economic, social, political, cultural and religious realities of the countries concerned. All of them are not concerned anyway, because much depends on the threat that the country in question poses to the West (economically most of the time, but sometimes, we have to admit it, militarily too) and on its alliances, pragmatism obliges. Once again this is understandable, as a cause can be served in many ways.

But let us come back to the subject of the chapter. China has never been a fundamentally egalitarian country (anyhow it would be difficult to find one, the search for equality is generally the last of the problems to be addressed, a somehow 'rich problem') but has never been a fundamentally unequal country either, unlike other countries still locked in a very heavy social straitjacket (I think of India, always confronted with the problem of castes in our 21st century, with an impermeable social system and an almost impossible caste ascent, despite all the major positive changes that have occurred in recent years). Moreover, if China has remained outside the philosophy of enlightenment (promoted by the 'philisophes des Lumières' in France in the seventeenth century) and the principles of democracy for quite a long time, the Chinese culture has never felt any lack in this respect, as its own cultural references were rich enough to be self-sufficient. Without these ideas from the West, we could imagine that China would have gone from a medieval or feudal system to an autocratic system, leaving little room for the individual in either case. This is absolutely not the case. China is a country whose culture is in fact quite balanced between the notion of group and the notion of individual. Social ascent has always been possible. As soon as the seventh century of our era, when the whole of Europe was barely entering the feudal age after the fall of Rome and the great barbaric invasions, there were already imperial exams to determine, among the population, who would be able to become the senior officials governing the State. The exams, probably inspired by the social and political philosophy of Confucius and for which any literate person could take, were a cog in the meritocracy because they favoured social ascent and equal opportunities for all (assuming that the individual had been able to receive an education and prepare it). Admittedly imperfect, the system had the merit of existing and it was probably unique of its kind at a time when equality was far from being considered as a global value. On this point, maybe China has greatly influenced other countries by giving the example, France being one of them, with the still current system of public service and high schools ('grandes écoles') exams. These exams indeed recall the spirit of the imperial exams brought back from China by the Jesuits and institutionalized, it is said, by Napoleon Bonaparte who, among other things, sought to replace the elite of the former regime by using an objective and less socially reproductive basis.

But where do we stand today? Is the country, through its current political system, so unequal that we want to portray it? How to situate it in relation to other nations in the world? To this end, there is a whole battery of indicators measuring social inequalities. Among them, the income share of the top 10% of the world's wealthiest people is a very interesting factor which allows to determine the first decile of income in the entire population and draw comparisons by countries or geographical areas but also over time. According to the data base of the WID (World Wealth and Income Database), quoted in a study on global inequalities directed by Thomas Picketty and published in December 2017, this share of 10% of the wealthiest global incomes was for about 42% of them in China at the end of 2016. It seems enormous, but China, here, was doing better than Russia (46%), the States and Canada (47%), and much better than India (56%). Only Europe was doing a little better at about 38%, a level that was growing in line with the global trend but at a very moderate pace. So, this is a good point for pour old nations, marked by the principles of redistribution, France being probably one of the leading countries in this field despite the complaints of its inhabitants.

According to the data base, we can notice that, at the beginning of the 1980s, countries with a leftist or Marxist doctrine like China or Russia (then USSR) were doing much better than the others: 21% for USSR and 28% for China, whereas Europe, India and the USA were in a pocket handkerchief with a similar level at about 33%. It was normal, but more than a positive point via a redistribution of wealth, I consider it's the consequence of a blockage in the level of high incomes coupled with the absence of large groups capable of generating profits. Therefore, it was an economic desert excluding the largest number of people. Then great upheavals occurred. Since Deng Xiaoping the Chinese economy has liberalized, opened to the world and the share of high incomes has increased from 1980 to reach a peak of about 43% at the end of the 2000s. Meanwhile the share of 10% of high incomes in Russia had exploded, starting from 25% in 1990 and reaching more than 50% in 2008, after the fall of communism and the monopolization of many resources by oligarchs, an effect reinforced by corruption. However, when inequalities still seem to be slowly increasing in the other countries (except Russia), apparently China contains these inequalities (here the figures speak for themselves). Is the coming to power of Xi Jinping, with the spearhead its anti-corruption policy, involved in this? It's difficult to check it, but we cannot deny the beneficial effects of his action and that of his government. The picture of glaring inequalities in China doesn't seem so black at first sight when looking at the other major economies. After observing the evolutions in different parts of the world, it's also interesting to see that increasing the level of human development and economic maturity doesn't necessarily mean reducing inequalities even if there seems to be a correlation.

Today in China we can really see inequalities more glaring than in Europe, but not much more than in the USA, and much less than in other developing countries (in South Asia particularly) or countries with a high human development index like the Gulf countries where poverty and luxury usually coexist.

In France, too, the vision of poverty in big cities like Paris is more and more present. The public is getting used to it and it might almost seem normal, which is terrible, with homeless people begging at the bottom of beautiful buildings at 10k to 20k euros per square meter. It's not so different from the situation in big Chinese towns where begging is less visible however (maybe a consequence of removal policies, much like in the central London area). On the other hand, real disparities in China are to be found in the opposition between developed towns (in the east) with the same (and sometimes higher) standard of living as in some parts of the West, and downgraded villages in remote rural areas, where the standard of living can be compared with that of a low-income African country. Let's note here that, in France, sad to say, the situation seems to be evolving in this direction, with a two-speed economy between the major cities and downgraded rural areas excluded from globalization.

The economic development, (especially if it is rapid and at an early stage), generates large fortunes. If China has been able to lift hundreds of millions of people out of poverty (many sources mention 700 million people at least) it's through the necessary enrichment of a few. This requires the control of a strong enough state to avoid a transfer of power to the big fortunes and large industrial groups, as in other countries close to China with the constitution (limited later) of an all-powerful class of oligarchs. In China these oligarchs exist but the big difference is that they are often members of the party and directly linked with it; it's a system that, despite real constraints, has the intelligence to avoid many conflicts of interest. In a context of rapid enrichment of only a few, as a first step it will also be necessary to avoid corruption, syndrome of social blockage of the largest number of people in favour of a small caste that will be challenged and will generate social movements in a position to become uncontrollable, whatever the political regime may be anyway. On this point, work has undoubtedly been done for several years now by Xi Jinping's administration, even if accusations of targeting only opponents (members of rival factions of the Party) are often made in our media.

By spilling, the abundance benefited other citizens, and then benefited the entire economy through an increase in public and private investment, consumption, production, progress in education, in short, laid the foundation for a strong economy. The theory of runoff, as liberal as that of the invisible hand, therefore, applies very well to China as a strange paradox for a regime that was based on socialist principles at the height of the communist bloc. China is a strange country marrying opposites in apparent harmony. The same applies to the notion of inequality: in the same country very large fortunes cohabit with rural people on the verge of poverty, but nevertheless the state pays everyone a pension and provides free medical care, not necessarily the best or the most accessible, given the very large population (although France, with the deterioration of the public hospital is taking a similar path despite great humanist speeches and increasing public spending), but which here again have the merit of existing. This is rather rare in fast developing countries and a comfort generally reserved for those who have become richer for a longer time. The social protection system in China has developed very fast: barely 20 years after the country's opening at the end of the 1970s-beginning of the 1980s. It rests on 5 pillars in its revised form in 2011: old-age insurance, unemployment insurance, health insurance, industrial accidents and maternity insurance. Still incomplete, these insurances benefit more and more Chinese people: the basic health insurance coverage rate was almost 100% in 2012 according to the National Bureau of Statistics in China. The basic old-age insurance coverage was more limited, neighbouring only 60% of the population according to the same source. For the other three pillars of Chinese social security the coverage rates were between 45% and 55% of the population in 2012 but they have since evolved in the right direction. As in France for instance, benefits are provided through contributions paid by the working-age population. The retirement age, which will change as the age pyramid shows signs of ageing, is set at 60 years of age for men and 55 years for women, with reductions at 45, 50 or 55 years for strenuous manual work. Now last but not least, there is a minimum wage for a legal working week of 40 hours: in 2017 according to the Centre for European and International Social Security Links it reached 2,190 yuans in Shanghai and 1,720 yuans in Beijing (about 250/300 euros per month, very little it seems, but displayed here without taking into account the cost of living, even if Shanghai and Beijing have unfortunately become very expensive). Average wages in 2017 are of course higher: 7,086 yuans in Beijing (about 900 euros) and 5,939 yuans in Shanghai (about 760 euros). This is far from the image of slavery that some people want to convey about Chinese labour, even if life isn't easy and abuses still exist. Although still insufficient, especially for rural households, social protection nevertheless exists and this reduces inequalities accordingly. Rich households will of course always be better off, everyone knows it and it would be difficult to be otherwise, but a social security base, however imperfect it may still be at this stage, allows the poorest to benefit from vital care and it's already a major victory when you see where China comes from and how quickly it has recovered, at the cost of great sacrifices.

All this being said to break a little the image of this China which would make fun of its population and would be the most unequal country in the world, which is far from being the case, I don't think that the fight against inequality at all costs is a policy to be implemented as a matter of priority. Naturally this is my opinion, but I am in favour of equality and not egalitarianism. It's not shocking that someone working more, better or who has been better trained or educated, can have a better life than their neighbours working less or taking fewer professional risks, just as it is normal for a boss, who undertakes and offers work to employees, to have a better salary and can own a larger part of his company. If it is necessary to ensure equal opportunities as much as possible so that everybody can achieve success according to their abilities (though total equality of opportunity is clearly a utopia, except by abolishing families, inheritances and physical characteristics), inequalities mustn't disturb us as long as they are not indecent and don't lead to social unrest. Everyone must have their fair share according to their work and talent, but complete equality is both senseless and undesirable. The only examples of it are equality in poverty, except for a few caciques, as in North Korea today or elsewhere in the recent history of USSR, in Cuba or other countries that tried to impose communism through their regime, against the natural character of human beings.

15. "WE DON'T UNDERSTAND ANYTHING ABOUT CHINESE CULTURE, IT'S FOLKORE

In a previous chapter concerning another preconceived idea, we have already mentioned the image of the Chinese dating back to the last imperial dynasty. When we talk about China, for some people it's still this image that first comes to their minds, mixed with some communist hints of Stalinist style from another age. This is, of course, an image very different from reality, a little like the image of the dirty Frenchman, a baguette under his arm, with a red nose from acne rosacea, wearing a 'marcel' shirt and peasant style braces from the 1940s, which comes to the minds of some Americans with similar representations blocked in the past.

In fact, in France and in Europe, our representation of China is often outdated, or even completely misleading. These images are well reflected in the food. Let's take the example of "lucky cakes", which you probably know, those little biscuits sometimes given at the end of a meal by your server in a restaurant supposed to be "Chinese". They are dry and hollow, and inside you can find a message telling what may happen to you in a near future or giving some general advice for the year to come. It's rather funny and looks very typical. However, most of the Chinese I have met had never seen this before coming to France, or before visiting the best-known Chinese districts in the West, like London or San Francisco (where I personally discovered the lucky cakes at the end of the 1990s). These cakes are a folklore that no longer represents Chinese culture at all; by the way, they are made in

Europe and no longer in China where it hasn't been practiced for a long time. It's always funny with the so-called Chinese districts to see that they are locked in time compared to continental China. In France many people will suppose they are sharing a typical Chinese meal when, at dessert or coffee time, these cakes are brought to them, but, in reality, there's a good chance they will be in a restaurant run by Vietnamese born in France, and they will call "Chinese meal" specialities from South-East Asia like spring rolls. But, as, for a majority of customers the Chinese culture is a great mystery, they will think that these specialities are typically Chinese which will once again propagate confusions and preconceived ideas. On the other hand, the restaurant-keepers may be real Chinese who reproduce this outdated pattern because they know it's a folklore that uninitiated French people like, with the impression of living a typical experience which, in fact, doesn't reflect the reality of China today. It's a sort of vicious circle which contributes to distorting the knowledge of China by the people of the West. It's not mean of course, but not very meaningful either.

So, there's a twofold problem here: first the image and traditions of China imagined by the Westerners are fixed in the past. The second problem is the cultural porridge mixing everything related to Asia by simplification. We feel it particularly at the culinary level. On this point, however, things are moving slowly, especially in Paris or London, where real and very typical restaurants have recently opened, run by new generations of Asian immigrants, acting as ambassadors for a precise cultural region (restaurants with Yunnan or Sichuan specialities for Chinese people, real Ramen restaurants from Hokkaido or from the south of the archipelago for the Japanese, or true Korean restaurants where they don't just serve bibimbap). Smart consumers make the difference and seek authenticity and modernity, not a parody of Asian culture.

But in the rest of the French territory you will always find "any type of food" restaurants serving, to please consumers, everything and anything under the "China" label: spring rolls, sushi, pork with caramel (the simplest and best-known dishes) or grilled kebabs. Of course, this creates a persisting confusion, exactly as if, in foreign countries, a restaurant presenting itself as French served burgers, spaghetti, cassoulet and mixed all the European cultures: it wouldn't make any sense. However, in 2018, strange as it may be, many people still think that sushi and sashimi are Chinese specialities, that the spring rolls are the national dish and the Chinese dessert par excellence is nougat (small pieces of tender sesame nougat) served in Europe but totally abandoned in China since the 1980s (you can just find this in Thailand today). Most of European consumers, even educated people, think there are no desserts in China and that the Chinese never consume sugar. Naturally this is inaccurate, and a large industry, specialized in cakes inspired by the West, has recently developed in the country, exactly like the Japanese pastry cooks who have been able to learn Western codes and now every year provide a contingent of pastry chefs, among the best of their generation. In China we can even find cakes unknown in Europe, very original and close to what can be found in the United States. Our old France no longer has the privilege of dessert and is inspired by China and Asia, as is the case with the incorporation of more and more products from the Asian culinary world into the preparations of our French top chefs.

In fact, when you look at it carefully, there are in Europe and North America gigantic persisting confusions on China and Asia in general. The West has created a kind of Asian cultural mixture which comes from a bad knowledge of Asia and the very marked cultural differences between the various countries, which has given birth to a real cultural melting-pot without much sense, a sort of grotesque patch-work created from scratch by the West.

The expression "Asiatic" we can hear more and more frequently ('Asiate' in France's newspeak) shows rather properly the emerged face of the iceberg about the remarks made above. It reveals the confusion that consists (out of ignorance or lack of interest) in putting into the same bag everything coming from Asia. Mr So and So is an "Asiatic", I go to an "Asiatic" restaurant. The expression creates somewhat borderline amalgams and continues to reproduce confusion by drowning China and neighbouring countries in a large group without distinction as well as their inhabitants.

I find it regrettable. Of course it's meaningless asking everyone to be opened to the world and interested in other cultures, even if they are thousands of years old and often full of wisdom (exactly like our own cultures or Greek and Latin influence, once more there is no value judgement in these statements), but it would be good not to constantly mix everything up. China knows the West better than we do and, one day, this will be detrimental to us (and probably to both parts) because a balanced relationship is built on knowledge and mutual respect. If we relegate others to the background because they are too different and live too far from us, or because of preconceived ideas (which can be observed in both directions), we'll collectively run the risk of missing out on one part of humanity on which, on the contrary, we could rely to exchange and progress.

However, things are changing rather quickly, and it's a real statement of optimism I make. China is becoming more visible. Not necessarily for the best, particularly in media, always quick to exaggerate to boost their audience and sell paper or advertising space, or still in the mouths of some politicians looking for scapegoats or populist diversionary subjects (and they are not always the ones we believe). But China is also more visible in everyday life. When walking in Paris we can notice the dynamism of the Chinese community and Asian nationals in general. In two decades the population has gradually changed: first exclusively coming from Southern Asia with a few Japanese and Korean nationals, then a disadvantaged Chinese population and a community very present in the catering and textile activities, and finally today we are witnessing the rise of a qualified generation deeply involved in the French economic fabric, which enables the development of Franco-Chinese exchanges (even after relocations in China) via investments (both in tangible and intangible assets) or the contribution of this French culture that make us proud on Chinese soil.

Among French people I also notice more and more curiosity, less and less full of commonplace. They are getting interested in Chinese traditions and festivals, especially at the time of the Chinese New Year (with the traditional family meeting and the return to the "laojia", the house in the family's region of origin) or other celebrations like the mid-autumn festival (15th day of the 8th lunar month, generally at the beginning of October) which is the second in importance in the Chinese calendar, when people consume "yuebing" (literally "moon cakes") , a tradition dating back to the Tang era about 1,500 years ago. The Chinese calendar is rich with many celebrations expressing various beliefs with particular (and tasty) cooking specialities.

Such a variety may seem a bit complicated but, as soon as you can make the difference (and it can be done quickly), stop mixing countries (Korea, Japan, China, Thailand, and so on) and so stop denying differences, all the cultural dimensions become highly interesting because they have a history and values. Moreover, they can be compared with the traditions of our old Europe which also benefits from a thousand of years old history, and, to my mind, this can really bring us closer together.

I won't go further in the description of Chinese festivals and traditions as this is not the subject of this essay. The very simple message of this part, which can also apply to other countries, is: let's get out of our Western prism, we know many traditions of our neighbours, we are soaked with American culture, we don't mistake Germany for Spain, and now that Asia is taking off, it would be good to know a little better those people who become our trading partners, our technological competitors, our diplomatic peers. All that can be done for a better mutual understanding is desirable, when tensions between the powers of a new multi-polar world are high and, we can learn from the past, in which most conflicts were generated by mistrust resulting from misinterpretations of our opponents' intentions. This knowledge is based on popular culture too, because, in fine, it is the people that represents the essence of nations and, consequently, their souls; the 21st century is the century of exchanges, and globalization, whether we like it or not. China has understood it well, and it is opening up while protecting itself. The time of a uniform Western culture is over, as well as the soft power which is also today the prerogative of other nations among which China is in the first place. The evolution of the world culture will be the guarantee of the multi-polarity of the world to come, and I am convinced that, in a near future, popular knowledge about China will match that of other developed countries we have known better for a long time.

16. "CHINA'S GROWTH IS BASED ON COPYING AND POOR QUALITY"

China only produces poor quality "junk stuff": this may be one of the most frequent criticisms that people make of Chinese products and China in general.

It has often been true in the past, when the country, at the beginning of its expansion and to recover economically, focused on low value-added production resting on a derisory labour cost, compared to the West, in order to increase its price competitiveness. And it worked well for decades. When I was a child in the 1980s or 1990s, I remember all the "made in China" printed on plastic toys. There were still some "made in Italy" or "made in France" but most of them have now disappeared. The Chinese giant had woken up, helped by the insatiable appetite of European and American consumers for low priced goods. It's a strategy that is still working fairly well today for some productions (even if China has a higher labour cost nowadays and is starting to delocalize in other South Asian countries), but the heart of Chinese economy has now turned towards technology. More and more Chinese quality products can be seen on the European market. It started with domestic appliances and brands like "Haier", then television or computer screens in the 2000s with "Lenovo" for instance, followed by the car industry (in this case mainly limited to the Chinese market), lastly the emergence of web giants and applications like "WeChat" by Tencent, (then very ahead of their time because combining the equivalents of Facebook, Twitter, WhatsApp and Apple Pay in a single application) or the messaging system "qq". Then there was the overwhelming Chinese domination in solar panels. Today there are different ranges of smartphones with Huawei, first of all, which creates models as powerful as Apple or very similar but at a lower price. In a more low-cost version, there are also "Xiaomi", "Honor", 'OnePlus", "Meizu" and others. In a near future, maybe we'll buy Chinese trains (in China high-speed trains are often as comfortable as the Shinkansen, and more than the French TGV, and, by the way, always punctual, without mentioning the price per kilometre which is quite interesting, but this concerns the railway operator and not the equipment manufacturer), industrial equipment, turbines, spatial equipment, not to mention the entire Chinese financial sector (banks and insurance companies) which is expanding at an unprecedented rate. The program of the civil aircraft manufacturer "Comac" is still in its infancy, but it may be able to compete with Airbus and Boeing in the future, even if it must take some time. The first commercial airplane of Comac is on the verge of being approved for commercial use at the end of 2019. All this is made possible by China's economic nationalism, the price of Chinese products much lower when compared with great Western brands, and also the critical size of the Chinese market: their products can be tested internally and manufacturers have the opportunity to develop and strengthen their brands before embarking on the conquest of non-domestic markets.

So, we could be in the situation to buy, consume, invest more "Chinese" if nothing is done to enable our industry to remain competitive, and, above all, if we always focus on price in the short term. A little intelligent protectionism coupled with targeted investments to preserve national industrial flagships, won't challenge the principles of free trade. China has always done it and it's a good strategy that works as we can see.

Donald Trump blames the theft of industrial property. Yes, we can't deny it, there are a lot of examples of copying or counterfeiting of foreign emblematic products, particularly luxury goods, made in China by unscrupulous companies. But counterfeiting is illegal and creates a risk for the country as international laws provide for strict sanctions, particularly in the chapters dedicated to the fight against counterfeiting defined by the WTO. So today, Westerners' criticism of China focuses on another subject: technology transfers; it is true that, attracted by the enormous potential of the Chinese market, concentrating more than a billion consumers, with a middle class that is getting stronger every day and have an increasing purchasing power, Western companies are constantly looking to establish themselves in the country. To protect itself and bring out national champions, China has imposed joint ventures on Western companies seeking to establish themselves on its territory. Thus, an automobile manufacturer will have to create a joint venture with a Chinese local manufacturer who will hold the majority of the shares, i.e. 51%. So we blame the Chinese for learning foreign technologies through this process and, in the end, for no longer needing Western companies to manufacture high value-added products. It is smart and fair game, but this approach has always been criticized and is part of the grey area of free trade law. Anyhow it permitted China to ensure a transition from low-cost to much more technical production and created real internationally competitive conglomerates, whether in information and communication technologies, automotive, engineering, construction, rail, aerospace or nuclear sectors. On the strength of this knowledge, Chinese groups are now ousting European groups on other markets, as in Africa, because they are now playing in the same court and can often still offer competitive prices. History repeats itself, but in a different direction: China hasn't forgotten the last two centuries when the West imposed its products and methods in Asia, which had ruined the country and its population.

Anyway, it's interesting to observe, once again here on the economic level, the paradoxical reactions of the West towards Chinese products. A large proportion of the population thinks that Chinese products have a poor quality. For some of them it's really the case, but we must consider their price: what can be expected of products that are 2 or 5 times less expensive? Is a similar quality possible? This is utopian and consumers sometimes demand it without rhyme or reason. The governments and consumers of many European countries (true for the United States too) also warn against Chinese products that are, according to them, responsible for the national trade balance deficit. This is the paradox: citizens complain but often choose the cheapest products. By their choice they create unemployment in their own countries, as the most expensive products (because of a labour-cost that is still very different between China and European countries) are abandoned in favour of imports at lower prices. Shooting with red balls at Chinese products, claiming their poor quality and buying them because they are cheaper, while complaining about unemployment in France and trade imbalances are attitudes difficult to understand, but consumers don't mind the paradox. Even if it's true, sad to say, that a part of the population can't afford the luxury of having access to more expensive European products. Everything is linked and the poverty rate is linked with the employment rate and the labour remuneration: if some productions were relocated back to our countries, there's a good chance that our fellow countrymen had a higher purchase power. It's a virtuous circle in short. Again, the United States are moving forward. But it seems the European Union is also beginning to understand these basic economics.

Then, for productions with a higher added value, our governments (and consumers too) blame China again for its economic expansionism. They will no more speak of "poor quality" or "low-cost production", though prices here are still often very competitive, but China will be blamed for something else: unfair competition, copying, economic pillage, appropriation of trade secrets made possible by the mandatory creation of joint ventures. In fact, I think we aren't yet used to being put in competition by Asian companies (other than Japanese of course, which were blamed for the same reasons in the 1970s and 1980s about the quick expansion of the Rising Sun Empire, when we then thought we would be slowly devoured, as suggested by popular culture, which is shown in some parodies by "the Strangers", "les Inconnus" in France, at the beginning of the 1990s), or losing markets. Economic battles are harsh, and all countries try to win them, sometimes using brutal or unconventional methods like a gradual devaluation of domestic currency, selective custom duties, a legislation that hinders foreign companies or a discriminatory tax or legal framework. China may have already used such schemes, but like other countries as the United states, according to journalistic sources, in the Alstom-General Electric case (in which several actors mentioned pressure on public and private decision-makers to sell a European company to an American group). Once more, China seems to be a scapegoat on this subject. As always, nothing is totally white or black, there is a part of both like Ying and Yang, and we must keep reason. I am confident in the fact that this globally negative vision of the country will eventually evolve in public opinion as the new world order is normalized, following the example of today's Japan which had been vilified by the West at the end of the 20th century. However, I do have some concerns: what if Japan's normalisation was due to the fact that it has been an ally of the Western bloc since 1945, therefore much more easily tolerable and controllable with an army that is non-existent if not extremely limited? Japan now asleep is not a threat to the interests of great powers, except, maybe, via its massive American debt holding, but it's not in the interest of Japan to cause a rate shock. Economics, politics and the military are sometimes closely linked. This may be weighing on China today, as it doesn't follow the trajectory that some would have liked. No one can tell now, but we'll see it clearly in the future. Anyhow, these subjects are fascinating; they go beyond the simple economic level and have a gigantic strategic and geopolitical dimension. It's clear today that globalization doesn't lead to total standardization and that multiple forces are in constant competition. All the countries that can do so, whatever they are, use a wide range of means, some of them being asserted, some others less respectable.

BONUS CHAPTER - "CHINESE PEOPLE LIVING IN FRANCE/EUROPE ARE RICH AND DISCREET"

As a conclusion to our chapters on preconceived ideas, let's now move away from Sino-Chinese subjects, for a good reason. It's probably one of the most important clichés towards our compatriots of Chinese origin (and more widely of Asian origin, as they are often generally assimilated to "Chinese") or Asian / Chinese foreigners living in France. It's a difficult subject because these clichés are favoured by cultural traits that can't be fully denied. Everybody won't probably agree with the following lines, but I think they reflect the feeling of a majority of Chinese or more widely Asian people living in France or Europe (mainly with the exception of the UK where I feel integration is often easier), regardless of nationality. We must also give another importance to the subject: these people of Chinese origin, through the links that unite them to both France and China, are very important ambassadors of French/Chinese relations or even Europe-China relations. It is therefore essential to understand, support and include them in our society.

This population is supposed to be "discreet, hardworking, withdrawn, self-reliant and accumulating money". Of these five terms two are meant to be compliments and the other three are more pejorative. But in all cases, even if they seem to be compliments (discreet, hardworking, respectful), we mustn't forget they are discriminating. The French of Asian origin or the Asians living in France do not have to be happy because the clichés they convey are more flattering than for other populations. Because the approach is the same: it's the generalization to each individual of characters perceived as common to a population. The individual's personality is denied here and reduced to a racial perception, and this is valid for any term, pejorative or not. These stereotypes have a particularly harsh life among people who, in the same way, will decry character traits perceived in other heterogeneous populations (Africans from black Africa, Arabs or Americans) and express condescension towards them. So, in my opinion, it's not because Asians are better perceived than other immigrant populations that we shouldn't denounce these clichés. By the way, as the conversation progresses, the positive terms may evolve very quickly into reproaches or even very negative or dangerous terms like "Asians live among themselves, they are rich, they steal from us, and besides they sell us their products at low prices and make us lose jobs". The border is thin: a cliché and discrimination remain a cliché and discrimination, whatever their meanings are. That being said, we mustn't fall into the opposite extreme and totally deny the cultural aspect. Common features from Asian culture can nevertheless be found and it takes them one or two generations to fade away as the roots become more distant between the country of immigration and the host country. About that the Chinese use the word "bananas" to speak of those who end up, through integration, being "yellow on the outside and white inside" (even more than the western natives in the end). But let's finish this digression.

In China, as has already been said, respect for elders is essential. This respect applies to families but also to all strata of society, and therefore, it is experienced as a shame not to be independent and to owe something to society. Therefore, Chinese families don't seek to take advantage of the welfare state and the children are educated through work very early in their lives. They are asked to be diligent and hardworking, to succeed and most will comply with it as that is what parents expect. So it's a fact that the work value is highly important for Chinese and many Asians. It's not surprising that their propensity to succeed socially and financially is higher than among other minorities, which, of course, strengthens clichés, negative this time, because success always attracts jealousy, especially in France, a free country but in which the eyes of others are unfortunately more often reproving than encouraging, and where money remains taboo, no matter how much it is, everything being relative.

Besides, Chinese families often help one another and especially their children, as said before. The unfailing support of the family circle is essential because it also promotes the success of children. The family still remains the foundation of Chinese society, a foundation we tend to forget in France, a country where the individual and the State seem to have become the two essential entities, which is in any case my perception.

So the Chinese are supposed to have more money, especially cash, which favours jealousy and aggressions. By the way this is not true, except sometimes for tourists who may hold cash on special occasions (purchases in department stores) or for Chinese traders or shopkeepers living in France who have some, like all traders in the course of their work. Chinese people or French of Chinese origin are much more visible nowadays than in the past because they have recently taken over many bars, tobacco shops, press kiosks, or restaurants. It is also a guarantee of integration into the local economy, in the same way as the conquest of the textile world nearly two decades ago.

However, the counterpart to this culture of work and family is detrimental to this category of the population: Asian/Chinese people are often considered by the rest of the population as being closed, quick to stay together and not very involved in social and political life. Once more, and this is what's both interesting and puzzling in clichés, there's a part of truth that generates them. I am sure it's not deliberate: people from Chinese families help one another a lot. How can we blame them, when the first generations arrived in France (those who generated the first clichés, and, of course I don't speak of the new presence of students or tourists who form separate groups) were confronted with a society that was not necessarily integrative with, in addition, difficulties to communicate in French. Mutual aid was therefore essential in everyday life. The fist immigrants coming from Asia and China didn't really choose to migrate, unlike today's arrivals that do so as part of their studies and settle in France according to their career opportunities. The generations arriving in the 1970s laid their bags in France (sometimes they had none) with everything to rebuild (many of them were refugees from the Indo-Chinese region and were often themselves descendants of Chinese lines) but kept a strong link with their culture, especially in cooking, which naturally gave birth to "Chinatowns" with people gathering together. Those typical districts are today quite fashionable in Paris for their cuisine and exotic products, to which other Asian worlds (Japan, Korea) have been added.

So all the ingredients are here to excite the imagination: a discreet, hard-working population with few demands: this is enough to stir up resentment in some people, who are occasionally awakened by cases of tax evasion (one of the criticisms often made on the spur of the moment). It's well-known: in France, only Asian restaurants forget to declare all their income of course, and nobody else is cheating! All this explains the prejudices of wealth, discretion and even of eviction of other populations in some areas or the control of this community over certain matters. Jealousy, when it comes to money, is unfortunately very easy to stir up and it's all the easier for a population that is hardly defending itself, not very concerned about politics and more focused on its business and the prosperity of its family.

But this "non-claim" rule has its limits and the red line is precisely the family. With the insecurity problems weighing on the Chinese community, reinforced by the prejudices we have just reviewed, some neighbourhoods became impossible and grumbling began to invade the streets. Chaolin Zhang's murder in august 2016, for a derisory loot of a few sweets and cigarettes, who (it is proven) had been targeted because he was Asian (once again based on the cliché "Asian means money and no defence"), was the tragedy of too much. It was followed by Shaoyao Liu's death, a Chinese national killed by the French police in March 2017 during a family dispute in troubled circumstances that even led to protests by the Chinese Ministry of foreign Affairs against France. Out of respect for families, no further comments will be made here, but what is certain is that, with these two cases, the compromises and the lack of consideration come to an end. The whole community took to the streets during demonstrations of a totally unprecedented scale to shout out their anger at being considered as a group of second-class citizens, and to show that they exist, which the French seemed to have discovered with astonishment without fully understanding the extent of the problem. It took tragedies, deaths, "lightning raid" operations from civil society for the authorities to finally begin to consider the problem. What's the population's main demand? It's protection. They don't ask for financial help, there's no struggle to maintain privileged status, no demand for more work, none of the above: only protection, the simple protection of people and property, which is one of the strictest attributions of the state in the regal sense of the term. And this protection, no matter what some people say, definitely exists in countries like China, Japan or Korea where weapons are forbidden, and deterrent sentences are applied to criminals.

France isn't basically a land of immigration, unlike North America or Australia. It's a country where republican values rest on the assimilation of foreigners into French culture, but it's slowly becoming a communitarian country, in the sense that several communities live side by side and less and less together. If vulnerable minorities are not protected, this trend will become more pronounced. How could the Asian community integrate socially (economic integration being already largely successful) into the Republic if they have to regroup to protect themselves and if they can't lead a normal life in some districts where local delinquency is fuelled precisely on prejudices of wealth, discretion and lack of complaint, which are relayed by French society ?

These considerations concerning the Chinese (as well as Asian) cultural characteristics are intended to be positive but often do more harm than good. I am convinced that this is a very unintentional clumsiness on the part of our compatriots who sometimes believe they are doing the right thing by seeking to value others and showing interest in their culture (or, more often, the culture of their ancestors), but, in doing so, they still convey these a-priori and make ethnic judgements denying the individual aspect which is reduced to its character and presumed culture, even if it's a second or third generation.

That's why I think that, without spending too much time on it, this particular prejudice, which is closely linked to France and less to China, has its place in this book. Without denying the important and often similar cultural aspects we can find among people of Asian cultures, we must realize that any generalization, whether negative or positive, leads to the formation of clichés that, sooner or later, contribute to the separation of the national community, an entity that is increasingly complex to understand and rationalize in a modern world where different cultures and colours coexist within the same country.

CONCLUSION: A GIANT LEAP

We have seen it throughout these few pages, China has defects like any country, some inherited from its history or the particularities of its regime, others created recently by the population's living environment. But let's not give in to alarmist sirens and let's not throw the baby out with the bath water. China is changing quickly and, despite this, the country still suffers from many prejudices as we have seen: Chinese people are supposed to eat dogs (there are probably more dogs consumed in Korea than in China but no one mentions it), to be impolite (are Parisians less rude, stressed out in a stifling capital as the people of Shanghai or Beijing can be?), and the Chinese would nurture the secret ambition of conquering the world (what recent war was provoked by China? What direct interference does China have in the affairs of third countries?).

In this book I have tried to redress what I consider to be a distorted view of reality by promoting a more objective reading of it, by explaining behaviours without judging them. We don't have to summarize in a few denigrating words or even a few qualities an entire culture and a whole country, in spite of the role of supreme judge some of us in the West have liked to play for centuries now. The Asian countries did understand it a long time ago. In the West we have a rich past made of many discoveries which have changed the face of the world and made our countries leaders. We still take pride in it today, even unconsciously, and we have imagined that we had a civilizing mission. Some benefits have obviously been brought to a large part of humanity, but this imperialist vision has also created deep imbalances. This page hasn't been turned yet, as evidenced by all these great speeches on the "universal values" of our political classes from all parties. In my opinion, however, we are mistaken if we persist in this path. We still have a lot to learn from other cultures that make up all the richness of humankind, and we have little legitimacy to judge them, no more than they have to judge our habits and customs. And even if Western values were ultimately perceived as being the best, confrontation will never be a good means to make countries with more authoritarian traditions move towards more liberal regimes, as we can see more and more clearly with Putin's Russia or Xi's China that is asserting itself in its alternative political model to the great displeasure of those who support uncontrolled liberality. I do hope that these few pages, in complete but always sincere, will open new perspective in our society and bring a small stone whose cluster may, one day, allow us to move towards a world where cooperation and exchanges will replace confrontation, mistrust and inappropriate moral lessons. But before that we must understand each other. That was the primary purpose of this book. With these few keys, everyone is free, to their own extent, to make this effort for a more optimistic future.

To return to China in particular, I confess once more that this book does little justice to Chinese culture. I simply wanted to let the readers know my hopes and doubts while sharing as best as I could what I have learned in a few years, and the shortcomings I can see every day in relations between the Far East and the West, shortcomings which are in no way limited to the simple roles of China and France and by extension of Europe. We often suffer from a complex of superiority over new powers or what we could call alternative powers (like Russia for instance, a real buffer between Europe and the Far East, and of course China whose stature has undergone an unprecedented transformation in just a few years). If we are not able to transform those differences in strengths, it might lead to serious crises. As a convinced European, I believe that Europe (via the European Union) has the potential to become the basis for cooperation between our western culture and the world's new economic train, Asia, whose bridgehead is China, as everyone can see today. Europe, with more pragmatism, can and must move closer to Asia and thus bring its voice of experience, stemming from millennia of History, to the concert of the global march of the world, a voice independent of all others, including the United States, even if this nation should remain our closest ally in the future. At a time when strategic interests between the major democracies are increasingly diverging and no longer allow nations to align themselves on this basis, let us hope that no new walls will be built between us.

In any case, this book has attempted to provide some simple keys with a general reflection on political, cultural, economic and social issues that affect us all in one way or another, regardless of our relationship with China, a large country of 1.4 billion inhabitants, more and more visible and who shouldn't frighten us. A lifetime wouldn't be enough to master the cultural richness of this country continent, at most it would serve us to appreciate its subtleties, but a simple little effort, a slight step towards more mutual understanding would, to paraphrase Neil Armstrong, probably be a giant leap forward.

December 2019

REFERENCES / SOURCES

- Jim O'Neill, *Building Better Global Economic BRICs*. Goldman Sachs, 30 November 2001. *Global Economics* n° 66

- Dominic Wilson, *Roopa Purushothaman, Dreaming With BRICs: The Path to 2050*. Goldman Sachs. *Global Economics* n° 99, 01 October 2003.

- Alexandre Kateb, *Les nouvelles puissances mondiales. Pourquoi les BRIC changent le monde*, Ellipses, Paris, 2011.

- Dominique Carreau, *Le Fonds monétaire international*, éditions A. Pedone, 2009, 200 p.

- Jean-Bernard Pinatel, article from Le Figaro, 09 January 2018

- Le Figaro : 03 October 2013 by Patrick Saint-Paul, « Les Chinois ne veulent plus passer pour des touristes mal-élevés »

- Lucien Bianco in collaboration with Hua Chang-Ming, « La population chinoise face à la règle de l'enfant unique », Actes de la recherche en sciences sociales, volume 78, 1989

- Le Moniteur du Commerce International, 2018

- World Wealth & Income Database (WID), 2017

- Jean-Pierre Duteil, "Le Mandat du Ciel : le rôle des jésuites en Chine, de la mort de François-Xavier à la dissolution de la Compagnie de Jésus, 1552-1774 », Paris, Arguments, 1994

- National Bureau of Statistics, Ministry of Human Resources and Social Security, People's Republic of China